The Last Stronghold
The Campaign for Fort Fisher

CIVIL WAR CAMPAIGNS AND COMMANDERS SERIES

Under the General Editorship of Grady McWhiney

PUBLISHED

The Last Stronghold
The Campaign for Fort Fisher

Richard B. McCaslin

McWhiney Foundation Press
McMurry University
Abilene, Texas

Library of Congress Cataloging-in-Publication Data

McCaslin, Richard B.
      The last stronghold: the campaign for Fort Fisher /
      Richard B. McCaslin.
      p. cm. – (Civil War campaigns and commanders)
      Includes bibliographical references and index.
      ISBN 1-893114-31-7
      1. Fort Fisher (N.C.: Fort)–Siege, 1864-1865. 2. Fort Fisher
(N.C.: Fort)–Capture, 1865. I. Title. II. Civil War campaigns and
commanders series.
      E477.28.M35 2003
      973.7'37–dc22

                                 2003015597
                                       CIP

McWhiney Foundation Press
McMurry Station, Box 637
Abilene, TX 79697-0637
(325) 793-4682
www.mcwhiney.org

Printed in the United States of America

ISBN 1-893114-31-7
10 9 8 7 6 5 4 3 2 1

Book Designed by Rosenbohm Graphic Design

A NOTE ON THE SERIES

Few segments of America's past excite more interest than
Civil War battles and leaders. This ongoing series of brief,
lively, and authoritative books—*Civil War Campaigns and
Commanders*—salutes this passion with inexpensive and
accurate accounts that are readable in a sitting. Each volume,
separate and complete in itself, nevertheless conveys the
agony, glory, death, and wreckage that defined America's
greatest tragedy.

In this series, designed for Civil War enthusiasts as well as
the newly recruited, emphasis is on telling good stories.
Photographs and biographical sketches enhance the narrative
of each book, and maps depict events as they happened. Sound
history is meshed with the dramatic in a format that is just
lengthy enough to inform and yet satisfy.

Grady McWhiney
General Editor

CONTENTS

CAMPAIGNS AND COMMANDERS SERIES

Map Key

Geography

 Trees

 Marsh

 Fields

 Strategic Elevations

 Rivers

 Tactical Elevations

 Fords

 Orchards

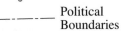 Political Boundaries

Human Construction

 Bridges

 Railroads

 Tactical Towns

 Strategic Towns

 Buildings

Church

Roads

Military

 Union Infantry

 Confederate Infantry

 Cavalry

 Artillery

 Headquarters

 Encampments

 Fortifications

 Permanant Works

 Hasty Works

 Obstructions

 Engagements

 Warships

 Gunboats

 Casemate Ironclad

 Monitor

 Tactical Movements

 Strategic Movements

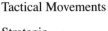

*Maps by
Donald S. Frazier, Ph.D.
Abilene, Texas*

MAPS

BIOGRAPHICAL SKETCHES AND PHOTOGRAPHS

The Last Stronghold
The Campaign for Fort Fisher

1
LIFELINE OF THE CONFEDERACY
WILMINGTON IN 1864

Col. William Lamb watched with grim satisfaction as hundreds of Union sailors and marines recoiled from the hail of gunfire hurled at them by his Confederates atop the northeast bastion of Fort Fisher. Suddenly, to his left he saw several flags planted by Bvt. Maj. Gen. Alfred H. Terry's Federal infantry on the far end of the parapets. Against these intruders, Lamb's district commander, Maj. Gen. William H.C. Whiting, led a counterattack that abruptly ended when he was shot. Lamb organized a bayonet charge as a last attempt to expel the bluecoats but fell wounded before it began. Laid next to Whiting in Fort Fisher's bombproof hospital, then carried to nearby Battery Buchanan, Lamb realized his fort was lost. It was the evening of January 15, 1865, and the last "lifeline" of the Confederacy had been cut.

Fort Fisher guarded Wilmington, which by 1864 had become an important target for Federal military planners because it was the primary haven for blockade runners in the eastern Confederacy and a base of operations for commerce raiders. It served, as many students of the war later noted, as the principal remaining supply source for the eastern Confederate armies. This distinction, which came because of the city's location and the configuration of its harbor, proved to be a mixed blessing. During the Civil War, the formerly quiet port became the focus of a swelling tide of commerce that had a distinctly seedy aspect. Nevertheless, those who remained in Wilmington understood their role, and they were not eager to have it suddenly ended by a Federal invasion. To keep that from happening, they relied on a strong system of fortifications, the most formidable of which was Fort Fisher.

Geography made Wilmington ideal for blockade runners and commerce raiders. The city lay twenty-eight miles up the Cape Fear River, well protected from Union warships offshore. In addition, ships used two good inlets to the river on either side of Smith Island. The distance between these passages was enhanced by the intervention of Frying Pan Shoals, which projected twenty-five miles out to sea between them and forced the Federal fleet to patrol a line of at least fifty miles. While Wilmington was the farthest port from Nassau for the blockade runners, it was the closest to Richmond, where Gen. Robert E. Lee's Army of Northern Virginia struggled to sustain the Confederacy. Three rail lines linked Wilmington not only to the embattled capital but also to other Confederate forces in the interior of the Carolinas. The loss of the north end of the Petersburg Railroad in August 1864 cut the direct link between Lee's army and the port by way of the Wilmington and Weldon Railroad, but the city continued to supply his troops through a circuitous line farther west that had been built during the war.

Wilmington's location made it a successful antebellum port. In 1861 it was North Carolina's largest city, generating a modest profit from the marketing of such commodities as cotton, rice, lumber, and naval stores. The population of 5,202 whites enjoyed such amenities as a well-developed business district, an acting troupe that performed in a theater in the town hall, and a public library. A measure of their prosperity was reflected in the fact that there were 4,350 blacks living in the city, more than nine-tenths of whom were slaves.

The demands of the struggling Confederate army and closure of other ports by Union operations brought an increasing stream of commerce into Wilmington. The South had almost no industry to provide essential materials for its more than 800,000 troops, and so it had to rely on imports. At the beginning of the war, there were at least eight active Southern ports from which trade could be conducted, but most of these were soon rendered useless by the Federals. Union troops occupied Cape Hatteras and Port Royal in 1861, while New Orleans and Norfolk were captured and Savannah was closed in 1862. Charleston was invested in 1863, and the loss of Vicksburg

BLOCKADE RUNNER *LADY STERLING*

Built in Britain; iron-hulled, shallow-draft, side-wheel steamer; made multiple runs into and from Wilmington; Capt. D. Cruikshank, of London, tried to depart from Wilmington during October 1864 with only one of his engine's two cylinders in operation; intercepted by USS *Eolus,* which later participated in both bombardments of Fort Fisher in December 1864 and January 1865; shell set afire one hundred bales of cotton in the forecastle; engine tenders stayed at posts until vessel was hit nine more times and heat and smoke became overwhelming in engine compartment; ship and cargo brought $500,000 in prize court at New York; each Union seaman involved

in its capture awarded $2,000; officers received up to $23,000; U.S. Navy paid $135,000 for the vessel; refitted and recommissioned in April 1865 as the USS *Hornet;* sold in June 1869 to private owners for $33,000; renamed *Cuba;* used to convey supplies to revolutionaries in Cuba until seized by U.S. authorities at Wilmington in 1870.

that same year made it almost impossible to bring goods from distant Galveston. The closure of Mobile in August 1864 left only Wilmington, with which many blockade runners were already familiar by the second year of the war.

Estimates are that more than four hundred trips were made in and out of Wilmington by blockade runners during the war. Few were owned by Confederates; most had English or Scottish registrations issued to investors attracted by the potential of tremendous returns on their investment. A ton of coffee could be purchased in Nassau for $249 and resold at the dock in Wilmington for $5,500. Southern cotton could be had for three cents a pound and sold in Britain for a dollar a pound. The *Banshee* returned a 700 percent profit for its investors in just eight trips into and out of Wilmington. Bulk commodities were not the only source of profit: a bottle of gin cost $6 in Nassau and $150 in the South, providing ample opportunity for a savvy seaman to make a little extra income. Wages for the latter reflect profit margins; one smuggler claimed the monthly wage of a sailor on a blockade runner was $100 in gold, far more than the average soldier, while the officers made as much as $5,000 per voyage with plenty left for the investors.

With such high stakes at risk, blockade runners bought vessels designed and built specifically for their business. Cargo would be transported to Bermuda or Nassau and reloaded into lighter-draft, faster blockade runners for the run to Wilmington. Long and low, these vessels drew only a little water and were powered by high-pressure steam engines linked to side wheels or, preferably, twin propellers. Painted gray, stoked with smokeless anthracite coal, and equipped with collapsible masts, they usually traveled quite fast for the era and were virtually invisible on the ocean, especially on a moonless night. Few blockading vessels could overtake a runner in good condition on the open ocean, even when it was packed to the gunwales with valuable, and heavy, cargo. Those that were captured were often converted for use by the Federals in the blockade, and some served in the bombardment of Fort Fisher in December 1864 and January 1865.

Successful runs made millions of dollars for the owners, but the ships also provided much-needed supplies for the Confederacy. Pres. Jefferson Davis reported to his Congress that between November 1 and December 6, 1864, forty-three vessels arrived at Wilmington and Charleston. A supplemental report revealed that during the months of October and November 1864, these two ports had received more than 8.6 million pounds of meat, over 1.5 million pounds of lead, more than 1.9 million pounds of saltpeter, about 546,000 pairs of

BLOCKADE RUNNER *ROBERT E. LEE*

Iron-hulled, side-wheel, shallow-draft packet steamer; built in Britain; originally named *Giraffe;* purchased by John Wilkinson, agent of the Confederate government, in fall 1862 for £32,000; Wilkinson remained as captain; first came to Wilmington on December 29, 1862, carrying along with cargo more than two dozen Scots lithographers to work for Confederate treasury; vessel commissioned into Confederate navy under new name and continued as blockade runner; made run into Wilmington twenty-one times, carrying an estimated seven thousand bales of cotton worth $2 million in gold to European buyers; returned with cargoes that brought its offi-cers as much as $5,000 per voyage; carried Wilkinson and others to Canada in fall 1863 to organize unsuccessful attempt to free Confederate prisoners held at Johnson's Island; later under the command of Lt. Richard H. Gayle, captured in November 1863 while steaming from Bermuda to Wilmington with thousands of pounds of shoes, blankets, rifles, and munitions; sold to U.S. Navy by prize court for $73,000; recommissioned as the *Fort Donelson* and assigned to blockade duty; participated in bombardments of Fort Fisher in December 1864 and January 1865 under the command of Acting Master George W. Frost; decommissioned in August 1865 and sold to a private owner.

shoes, 316,000 pairs of blankets, 3.5 million pounds of meat, 520,000 pounds of coffee, 69,000 rifles, 97 packages of revolvers, 2,639 packages of medicine, forty-three cannon, and many other important items. Historians have estimated that nearly two-thirds of the Confederacy's weapons, one-third of the lead for its bullets, three-fourths of the ingredients for its powder, and most of the cloth and leather for uniforms and other equipment came from blockade runners.

The demand for necessary supplies and the lure of substantial profits attracted both the Davis administration, which invested in several blockade runners, and the state government of North Carolina. The administration of Gov. Zebulon B. Vance purchased a handful of runners, the best known of which was the *Advance.* That vessel, built in England, made its first run from Nassau to Wilmington in the summer of 1863 and made regular voyages until its capture in September 1864. After the war ended, Vance bragged that his agents had kept North Carolina troops well fed and clothed through the end of the war while generously sharing many supplies with their less fortunate comrades from many other Southern states.

Davis included Charleston in his report, but by late 1864 most of the material coming into the Confederacy from overseas came through Wilmington. The closing of Charleston to all but the most daring runners by a Federal land and sea operation forced many firms to move to Wilmington in the latter half of 1863. Charleston's misfortune was Wilmington's gain. In 1861 and 1862 there were only 7 recorded arrivals of steamers at Wilmington and just 4 departures during the same period. Charleston in those two years received twenty-seven steamers and sent out thirty-three. Arrivals skyrocketed at Wilmington in 1863 and 1864, when the numbers reached 128 and 164 respectively. At the same time, departures from that port climbed to 117 during 1863 and 179 in 1864. Charleston in the meantime withered under the attack on its harbor defenses, receiving only forty-six runners in 1863 and even fewer, thirty-one, during 1864. Departures from Charleston declined as well, to 49 in 1863 and 30 in 1864. All activity would end abruptly for both ports in 1865, but during the last year of the war, Wilmington enjoyed an almost six-to-one advantage in trade over stricken Charleston.

Wartime demands transformed business in the North Carolina port. Not only did many English companies establish offices in the city for blockade running, but there were other new enterprises as well. A steam press was built in a marsh outside the city to compress cotton bales so that more would fit in a ship. There were two large shipyards in the city, each of which constructed an ironclad warship and other vessels during the war. Too, there were important salt works in the vicinity of the city to take the place of those lost to advancing Union armies in upland regions of the Appalachians.

Wilmington also attracted the notice of the Federals when it became a haven for commerce raiders. Some prominent Confederates reported that these ships did little good and drew unwanted attention, but such complaints were ignored. The CSS *Tallahassee,* based at Wilmington, captured more than thirty vessels in the first half of August 1864, destroying twenty-six. Renamed the *Olustee,* she sailed again in November, sinking seven more victims along the coast of Delaware. That same month, the CSS *Chickamauga* captured seven vessels, burning six of them.

It was not just commerce that changed in Wilmington. While the city became busier, the quality of life declined noticeably. William Lamb, colonel of the 2d North Carolina Artillery and commander of Fort Fisher, remarked when he arrived that he found Wilmington to be a pleasant city. His wife also wrote that the people seemed to be mannerly and kind. However, in a short time the environment changed, and Lamb sent his wife, who was pregnant, to live with his family in Norfolk. When the Union army occupied that city and arrested Lamb's father, she moved again, this time to her parents' house in faraway Providence, Rhode Island. She did not return to Wilmington until after she had delivered a son, leaving him with her parents while she settled with her older children in a cabin built outside of the city and near the fort that her husband commanded.

The decline in Wilmington began when yellow fever ravaged the city during the fall of 1862. A blockade runner brought the disease from Nassau, and it devastated the town. The death toll exceeded 1,000 people, all of whom were buried in long trenches in Oakdale Cemetery, while six times that number fled to avoid a grim death. The epidemic ended with a heavy snowstorm during the first week of November. Those men who remained behind had plenty of work, while their wives labored to care for wounded soldiers who were brought to Wilmington and to provide clothes and other supplies for those at the front. They shared their city with disturbing new neighbors as many empty houses were occupied by strange tenants. Speculators and even more unsavory characters came to the city to make a fortune. Violent crime became common, while foreign- and native-born businessmen lived opulently. The free-spending ways of the latter drove prices out of the reach of many ordinary citizens: a dozen eggs rose from 15 cents a dozen to $10 a dozen, bacon from 25 cents a pound to $7 a pound, and a chicken from 25 cents to $12 apiece.

Wilmington by late 1864, when the blockade-running business was booming, had assumed a distinctly seedy appearance. Families who could afford to do so remained away from the city, while many men who stayed to tend businesses sent their wives and children to live with inland relatives. Formerly well-kept homes became vacant shells with peeling paint and dangling shutters, and the roads became filled with potholes. Wandering through the rutted streets and shabby homes were Confederate soldiers, crewmen from the blockade runners, and a mob of black and white dock laborers. The arrival of a runner or the announcement of an auction of the contents of such a vessel brought an eager rush of people into the streets seeking a bargain or to learn if their investment had paid as well as they had expected. Nevertheless, the city remained important to the Confederacy, and its denizens, however sad or unseemly, provided a vital service.

Recognizing the importance of Wilmington, Union blockaders sought to prevent ships from reaching the port since the summer of 1861, though to no avail. The first Federal ship, the *Daylight*, arrived in July 1861. This tiny vessel was soon disabled, but its place was taken by dozens of others as the North

Atlantic Blockading Squadron developed. By December 1864, thirty-three warships patrolled at Wilmington, posted in a double semicircle at the mouth of the Cape Fear River to cover both inlets. They managed to capture an increasing number of blockade runners that tried to slip in or out of Wilmington, but many eluded them. The zeal of the Federals for the chase was enhanced by the fact that crews shared the proceeds when a captured runner and its cargo were sold. Sometimes a sale meant as much as two thousand dollars for ordinary seamen, almost the equivalent of a year's wages.

Lee declared in late 1864 that if Wilmington was closed, he would have to evacuate Richmond. Federal officials knew this as well, and they began planning to block permanently the inlets to the Cape Fear River. But to do so would require much more than sending additional vessels to patrol offshore. The river itself would have to be occupied, and the city would have to be taken. Until that time, the needs of the Confederacy and the desires of speculators would ensure that blockade runners would continue to steam downriver in the dark, probing the cordon of blockaders for a gap that would allow them to escape into the open sea. Others would continue to come from overseas, watching in the night for the signal lights from Fort Fisher, guardian of the last lifeline of the Confederacy.

2
GIBRALTAR OF THE SOUTH
BUILDING FORT FISHER

To keep the Federal navy offshore and away from Wilmington, the Confederates built or refurbished six forts at the mouth of the Cape Fear River. Farther upriver were four more earthworks to guard the city from a Federal advance. Blockade runners preferred to slip into New Inlet, so the key to the entire system became Fort Fisher, which guarded that passage. Begun as a set of earthen redoubts, under the direction of Col. William Lamb this installation became the largest earthwork in the world. Many compared it favorably to the British stronghold that guarded the entrance to the Mediterranean Sea, calling it the "Gibraltar of the South."

The Confederates inherited a few forts at Wilmington, and they labored to improve them. Confederate and Federal engineers alike discovered that earthworks were more effective than masonry forts because the former could absorb an artillery bombardment that would reduce the latter to rubble.

Fort Caswell stood on the western side of Old Inlet, across from Fort Holmes on Smith Island. The former was a masonry post built by U.S. Army engineers thirty years before the Civil War began, while the latter was an earthwork thrown up by the Confederates. Near Caswell, also on the west side of the Cape Fear River, were Forts Campbell and Johnston, both of which were also earthen structures. Upriver, positioned to watch New Inlet, were two more earthworks, Fort Lamb on the western shore and Fort Fisher across the river. Above Fisher were four earthworks—Fort Anderson (west of Cape Fear River), Sugar Loaf, and Batteries Anderson and Gatlin (these three between the river and the Atlantic)—positioned to protect the approach to the city of Wilmington.

Fisher's location made it the focus of this collection of harbor defenses. The preferred route for blockade runners to slip into Wilmington was to steam north of the entrances to the Cape Fear River in the dark, then quickly slip south close to the shoreline, using the woods to mask their outline and the surf to muffle any engine noise. They looked for New Inlet, to the north of Smith Island and Frying Pan Shoals. Fort Fisher, whose bulk spanned the narrow peninsula between the Cape Fear River and the Atlantic Ocean eighteen miles south of Wilmington, guarded the entrance to New Inlet, keeping blockaders at bay and providing protection for runners. The spit of land on which Fisher stood had once provided a foundation for a government lighthouse and was known as Federal Point before the war, though after secession it was called Confederate Point. If Fisher fell, none of the other works would be of substantive value because the Cape Fear River would be closed to runners and the port would be worthless.

The diverse works below Wilmington were in various stages of construction or repair when Maj. Gen. William H.C. Whiting came to the city in November 1862 to take charge of the Third Military District. Fort Caswell's masonry walls had been masked with some dirt, and a line of earthworks had been dug nearby, but Fisher was little more than a scattering of redoubts. Whiting was an intelligent and experienced officer who realized that this would not do. The son of an army officer,

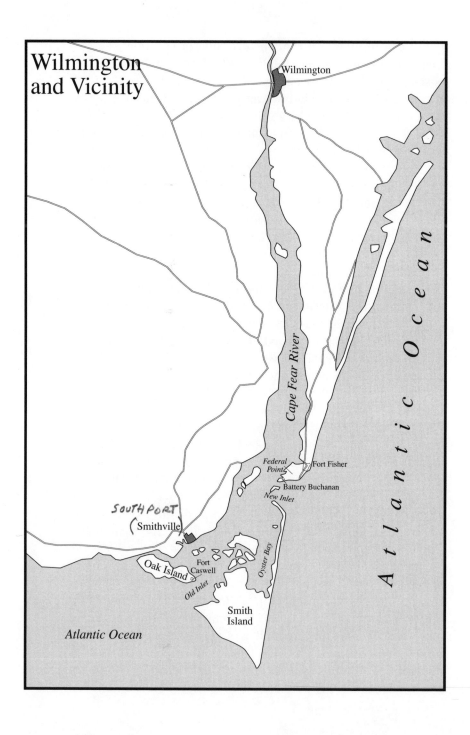

Wilmington
and Vicinity

Wilmington

Atlantic Ocean

Cape Fear River

Federal
Point

Fort Fisher

Battery Buchanan

New Inlet

SOUTHPORT
Smithville

Oyster Bay

Oak Island

Fort
Caswell

Old Inlet

Smith
Island

Atlantic Ocean

Whiting had finished a four-year course of study in two years at Georgetown University, then earned the highest marks ever recorded to that time as a cadet at West Point, from which he graduated in 1845. His prewar career was in the engineers, and during a tour of duty at Caswell, he married a woman from Wilmington. He did well as a brigade commander in Virginia, but a bitter feud with Pres. Jefferson Davis led to his transfer away from the front and to Wilmington. A chance to redeem himself at Petersburg in May 1864 went awry when he failed to trap some Union attackers, so he returned to Wilmington for the last time.

Whiting did realize that, despite its unformed appearance, Fisher was taking shape under the careful direction of Colonel Lamb, its commander. Lamb was born in Norfolk in 1835. His father was a successful attorney and sometime mayor of the city, so he paid to send his son to a Virginia military academy and a preparatory school in the North as well as to the College of William and Mary. After Lamb graduated Phi Beta Kappa with a bachelor of laws degree in 1854, his father bought an interest in a Norfolk newspaper and gave it to him. The younger Lamb became an active Democrat who hated Republicans, a sentiment shared by his Yankee bride, Sarah Anne Chafee of Rhode Island, whom he met when his family traveled north in 1857 to escape an epidemic of yellow fever in Norfolk. They married on September 7, 1857, his twenty-second birthday.

Lamb became involved in military matters as early as 1858, when he helped organize the Woodis Rifles, a Norfolk militia unit. Elected captain, he commanded his company at John Brown's hanging in 1859. He eagerly supported secession and led his company in a skirmish with a Federal gunboat less than a month after Virginia left the Union. Soon thereafter, the Woodis Rifles joined the 6th Virginia Infantry and Lamb, promoted to major, was sent to Wilmington to serve as the chief quartermaster for the District of Cape Fear. He was assigned to command some of the earthworks on the Cape Fear River soon after his arrival. He read books on military engineering as he worked, impressing superiors with his quickly acquired skill. In May 1862 he was elected colonel of the 36th North Carolina State Troops, which then mustered into Confederate service as the 2d North Carolina Artillery at Fort Caswell.

It became obvious that Lamb would be an excellent choice to take command of Fort Fisher and transform it into a more formidable position. At the age of twenty-six, Lamb became the post's commander on July 4, 1862. He arrived at the fort

WILLIAM H.C. WHITING

Born Biloxi, Mississippi, 1824; graduated with high honors from Georgetown College (Washington); graduated first in his class at West Point, 1845; joined Corps of Engineers and supervised construction projects in California and the South until he resigned as a captain 1861; planned defenses at Charleston; served as Gen. Joseph E. Johnston's chief engineer and earned a battlefield promotion to brigadier general at First Bull Run in July 1861; led a division at Seven Pines in May 1862, in the Shenandoah Valley in June 1862, and during the Seven Days in June and July 1862; revered by his troops, who called him "Little Billy," though superior officers were disappointed with his sluggish combat performances; transferred to command Third Military District; major general, April 1863; returned to Virginia in May 1864 as commander of troops at Petersburg; failed to properly support operations against Benjamin F. Butler in Bermuda Hundred campaign and asked to be relieved after malicious reports surfaced that he was intoxicated on the field; returned to Wilmington and resumed command of district; present at Fort Fisher during Union attacks during December 1864 and January 1865; led counterattack along landface until wounded and taken prisoner on January 15, 1865; died in prison hospital on Governor's Island at New York on March 10, 1865.

about noon on that day and completed his first inspection by nightfall. Lamb's new command already had its name from Col. Charles F. Fisher, the popular commander of the 6th North Carolina Infantry who was killed at First Bull Run, but it could boast of little else. One recently erected earthwork, known as Shepherd's Battery, held two guns. Nearby was a square work

WILLIAM LAMB

Born Norfolk, Virginia, 1835; earned law degree from William and Mary in 1854; father, a former mayor of Norfolk, purchased half-interest in newspaper *Southern Argus* for him; served as delegate to Democratic National Convention in 1856; elector for John C. Breckinridge in 1860; militia captain beginning in 1858; led company at hanging of John Brown in 1859; company mustered into 6th Virginia Infantry; promoted to major and sent to Wilmington as a quartermaster officer; assigned to Fort Anderson on Cape Fear River; transformed that post into a formidable earthwork; transferred to Fort Fisher in July 1862 as colonel of 2d North Carolina Artillery (36th North Carolina State Troops); allegedly nominated for brigadier general but never confirmed; commanded Fisher during Federal bombardment in December 1864; again commanded Fisher during second Union attack in January 1865 until shot in left hip and carried to Battery Buchanan; captured and held at Fort Monroe in Virginia; remained on crutches for seven years; returned to Norfolk after the war; worked for Norfolk and Western Railroad;  became president of local utility company; delegate to Democratic National Convention in 1876; became a Republican sometime afterward; mayor of Norfolk, 1880–86; delegate to Republican National Convention in 1888; received honorary degree from St. Lawrence University; served as consul for Germany and Sweden in Norfolk; died March 23, 1909.

Interior of Shepherd's Battery, Fort Fisher

known as Fort Fisher that had six guns, two of which were large smoothbore Columbiads. A log work, Fort Meade, held four 8-inch smoothbore Columbiads. To the right of this was a small redoubt, known as Cumberland's Battery, that held a rifled gun capable of long-range fire. To its right were two small batteries, Hedrick and Bolles, each of which contained two guns "of moderate calibre." Bolles was actually the first emplacement built on Confederate Point in 1861. On Zeke's Island in New Inlet was a small battery with two guns; this work washed away and the guns were moved.

Lamb wanted to apply his new expertise in creating a magnum opus, a fortress so strong that it could survive any bombardment. He needed manpower to build his dream, and he directed as many as a thousand soldiers and slaves each day in the work of enlarging Fort Fisher. Until the fall of 1863, he was assisted by Maj. John J. Hedrick, his predecessor as commander of Fisher. Hedrick had come to Fisher with his artillery company, Company C (Cape Fear Light Artillery) of the 2d North Carolina Artillery, in late 1861, and he remained when the unit transferred away in April 1862. The major directed the labor of a handful of artillery companies until most were sent to nearby Smith Island in the fall of 1863 to be mustered as the 3d North Carolina Artillery (40th North Carolina State Troops), with Hedrick as their colonel. All of the companies of Lamb's 2d North Carolina Artillery, some of which had been at other works around Wilmington, subsequently gathered for the first time to work with others at Fisher. There they dug dutifully, if not happily, alongside dozens of slaves.

As completed, Fisher extended across Confederate Point, facing north, then made a sharp turn and continued south for 1,900 yards along the sea. The landface consisted of sixteen hollow mounds of sand covered with sod, inside each of which was a bombproof shelter connected to others by a passageway. Between the manmade hills, known as traverses to engineers such as Lamb, were large platforms that held a total of twenty pieces of siege-class artillery, most of which were gigantic smoothbore Columbiads. The traverses averaged thirty-two feet in height, and each was about thirty feet thick. The gun platforms were almost twenty feet in height, and the gunners were protected by walls about six feet high. Together, the gun platforms and the protecting walls were well over twenty feet in height, and they were twenty-five feet thick at the base.

Lamb did not rely only on the huge guns and piles of sand to defend Fisher's landface. Three large mortars and three Napoleon smoothbores, fieldpieces that threw a twelve-pound shell or ball, augmented the firepower of the larger pieces. Two of the light guns were positioned so they could be pushed through a sally port midway along the landface to an elevated position on an exterior palisade of sharpened pine logs nine feet in height. There was no break in this stockade except where the road from Wilmington intersected it near the Cape Fear River. At that point, a gate had been barricaded with sandbags to shield the third Napoleon. For greater protection against an infantry assault, two dozen mines were placed in the sand in front of the northern wall to be detonated with an electric charge from a battery inside the fort.

Exterior of Landface, Fort Fisher

Where the landface approached the sea was a taller traverse known as the Northeast Bastion. About forty-five feet in
height, it was more than a dozen feet higher than the mounds
that formed the landface. Adjacent to this was a semicircular
work known as the Pulpit, within which Lamb established his
field headquarters. Underneath this edifice was an immense
bombproof shelter designed to serve as a hospital. Too, there
was yet another sally port, protected by an 8-inch Blakely
rifled gun. Like the other cannon along the seaface, including
a huge 10-inch smoothbore Columbiad in the Northeast
Bastion, the Blakely was sited low for ricochet firing across
the water. Behind the Northeast Bastion and the Pulpit was
the post's main magazine, a huge bombproof shelter contain-
ing 13,000 pounds of black powder. From his vantage point
atop the Pulpit, Lamb could see the entire landface as well as
down the seaside front all the way to Battery Buchanan, which
lay more than a mile away. A buried telegraph line linked him
to the southern end of his fort and with Wilmington to the
north.

The seaface was almost a duplicate of the landface in its
design, but it was much greater in length. Two dozen siege
guns were placed on the platforms between the hillocks facing
the sea. Like those on the northern wall, the cannon facing the

Interior of Seaface, Fort Fisher

sea represented a variety of technologies, some of which were quite advanced. Midway along the seaface was an Armstrong rifled gun capable of throwing a 150-pound shell for well over two miles. A gift from a British industrialist, this piece had a mahogany carriage with bright brass fittings. It provided a suitable, if showy, partner for the Blakely gun at the Northeast Bastion, which had also come from Britain. Brought into Wilmington in 1863 by a blockade runner, the Blakely could hurl either a 170-pound shell or an immense load of canister from its bore. Also on the seaface were Whitworth rifled guns, British-made breechloaders that could throw a 12-pound bolt for five miles. Their accuracy forced Federal blockaders to keep a respectful distance. The first Whitworth had been salvaged from the wreckage of a blockade runner and proved effective as mobile artillery until it was lost in a lopsided duel with three Federal gunboats. As a result, the Confederates acquired several more and either installed them in the fort or rigged them with mule teams for mobile service along the shore.

Fisher's most imposing feature was the Mound Battery, which loomed sixty feet and anchored the southern end of the seaface. This earthwork took more than a year and a half to complete and required the construction of an inclined railway to carry sand to the top. On the peak were a 10-inch smooth-bore Columbiad, a 6.5-inch rifled gun, and a beacon to guide blockade runners, who could see this highest traverse for many miles out to sea. They sometimes referred to it as the Big Hill, and one, Capt. Thomas E. Taylor of the *Banshee*, recalled it as being "about as high as a full grown oak tree." When President Davis visited Fort Fisher in 1863, he was escorted to the top of the Mound Battery to receive a salute of twenty-one guns from the fort's garrison.

South of the Mound Battery and across a long expanse of sand stood Battery Buchanan, which shielded the southern end of Fort Fisher's seaface. Two stories in height, it boasted two 11-inch Brooke rifled guns, which were made in the Confederacy; a pair of smaller 10-inch Columbiad smooth-bores; and a Napoleon 12-pounder. Above Battery Buchanan, Lamb added a single line of rifle pits from the southern end of the seaface across at a northwesterly angle to the Cape Fear River. It was intended that this would help protect the fort from a Federal landing in the rear, though it did nothing to provide cover for garrison troops moving from Buchanan into Fisher. In an otherwise well-designed post, this did not seem important, but it would prove to be a problem.

The garrison of Fort Fisher lived outside the earthwork in huts and tents. It was hard to procure sufficient rations, and the supply of drinking water was limited and brackish. Exposed to extreme weather, which ranged from bitter cold in the winter to scorching humidity in the summer, the Confederates suffered from disease. Some of the latter undoubtedly came from the huge mosquitoes that preyed on the unhappy soldiers. Sand settled in everything. If the fort was attacked or besieged, the men would be sheltered in the bombproofs, which were sand floored and uncomfortably hot even in the winter but apparently impervious to shells. The troops could also huddle in the gun chambers upon the open platforms, but there they would be exposed to both the weather and gunfire.

Lamb's quarters were not much better than those provided for his soldiers. He conducted his daily business inside the fort

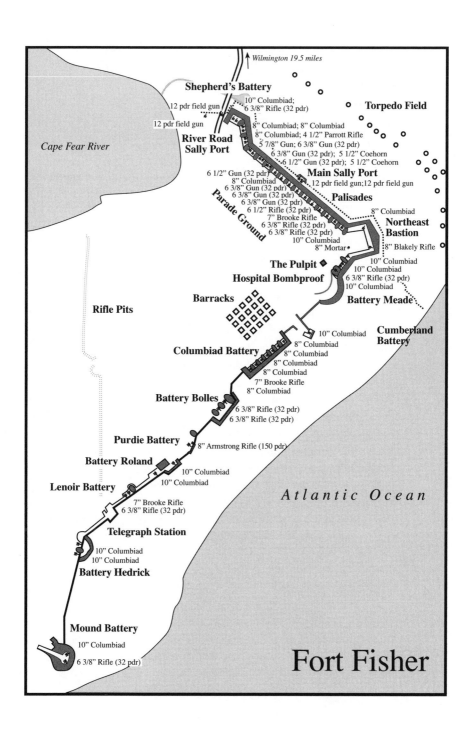

Fort Fisher

in a three-room brick house formerly used by the Federal light-house keeper, though the lighthouse itself had been disman-tled. The colonel lived with his wife and two children nearby. She had delivered their third child, a boy, on May 15, 1862, in Norfolk, shortly after the Union occupation. She accepted her father's invitation to return to his home in Providence, Rhode Island, but decided to join her husband at his post. Leaving her youngest child with his grandparents, and most of her clothing and other possessions with zealous Union inspectors who refused to let her pass with them, she traveled to Wilmington. The garrison built a three-room wooden cottage facing the beach a mile north of the fort, and Lamb planted peach trees and laid sod. There she and her husband lived and entertained distinguished visitors despite its exposure to occa-sional shells from blockaders offshore.

The garrison and workers at Fort Fisher learned that life under the direction of Colonel Lamb would be quite different than it had been under Major Hedrick. On the morning of his first full day, Lamb was astounded to see a Union blockader peacefully anchored within range of his artillery. An inquiry directed at a nearby subordinate elicited the information that the gunners had been told not to fire at the enemy unless they were fired upon first. Lamb angrily barked an order, and a shot fell near the Federals, who prudently moved away. Previously, Lamb learned, warships had occasionally shelled the workers from points well within range of the post's guns. Now the Federal fleet would keep a respectful distance from Fisher's guns, thus spreading out fur-ther and providing a better chance for the blockade runners as well as more security for the garrison.

Taylor, erstwhile captain of the *Banshee,* wrote in his mem-oir that Lamb "came to be regarded by the runners as their guardian angel; and it was no small support in the last trying moments of a run to remember who was in Fort Fisher." Lamb's persistent and ultimately successful opponent, Rear Adm. David D. Porter, later noted that the showing of any light by the Union fleet at night would bring a volley from Fisher. These shots he dismissed as more noise than danger, but he admitted that a hit would have demolished a Federal vessel.

Pursued blockade runners often breathed a sigh of relief when they heard the discharge of guns from Fort Fisher and the whir of shells overhead, for that meant pursuing blockaders would shy away rather than risk a hit. Once they were under the guns of Fisher, the runners knew they were safe.

Lamb's shells saved blockade runners from pursuit more than once, and at least one time boatloads of volunteers from Fort Fisher boarded a burning vessel (the *Night Hawk*) extinguished the flames, and saved it after her crew abandoned the ship. His garrison also recovered cargo from wrecks and combed the beach for jettisoned goods. One sad find was the body of the famous spy, Rose Greenhow. In October 1864, shells from Fisher dissuaded blockaders from pressing their attack on her ship, the *Condor*, but the vessel was grounded. Convinced that the surf would soon shatter the vessel, Greenhow insisted upon being taken ashore in a lifeboat. The tiny craft was swamped in the rough seas, and Greenhow, weighted down with gold, drowned. A soldier found her body on the sand north of the Mound Battery, but he looted the gold and ran away. It was Taylor who officially recovered the corpse and took it to Lamb's cottage, where the colonel's wife prepared it for burial in the city.

By December 1864, when the Federal fleet came to challenge his siege guns, Lamb had converted a motley collection of small redoubts into the largest earthwork in the world. Bristling with more than four dozen pieces of artillery, some of them of impressive caliber and range, Fort Fisher was well prepared to serve as a solid cornerstone for the defense of Wilmington, the primary port in the eastern Confederacy. Blockade runners relied upon the fort for protection from Federal blockaders, who in turn maintained a prudent distance from its guns. Without Fisher, the port would be bottled up and useless. Whiting was determined not to have the loss of Wilmington as the climax to a disappointing career as a Confederate officer. He relied upon Lamb and the defenders of Fort Fisher to make it so.

3
UNSURPASSED GALLANTRY AND SKILL
COMBATANTS AT FORT FISHER

On March 1, 1865, North Carolina representative Thomas C. Fuller introduced into the Confederate Congress a resolution of thanks to Maj. Gen. William H.C. Whiting and Col. William Lamb, as well as their men, for the defense of Fort Fisher. The resolution, which was approved unanimously, provided scant comfort for either commander or their troops. Crippling wounds confined Lamb and Whiting to their prison beds in Forts Monroe and Columbus respectively; Whiting died just nine days later. Their subordinates who had survived the Federal assault were also languishing in prison camps in New York or Maryland. The U.S. Congress had already approved a resolution of thanks to Federal forces by the time that their Confederate counterparts acted. On January 24, 1865, just nine days after Fisher fell, they praised Bvt. Maj. Gen. Alfred

H. Terry and his men for "unsurpassed gallantry and skill" in achieving a "brilliant and decisive victory." Both the outnumbered Confederates and the determined Federals richly deserved the gratitude accorded them.

Lamb had only his own regiment as a permanent garrison at Fort Fisher, and sometimes not even that. Fisher in December 1864 was defended by five companies of Lamb's 2d North Carolina Artillery: B (Bladen Stars), E (Columbus Artillery), F (Pamlico Artillery), H (Clarendon Guards), and K (Brunswick Artillery). Lamb was colonel of the 2d Artillery, but actual command fell to Maj. James M. Stevenson while Lamb tended to the fort. Stevenson followed Gen. Braxton Bragg to Savannah in November 1864 with five of his companies—A (King Artillery), C (Braddy's Battery), D (Anderson Artillery), G (Lamb Artillery), and I (Bladen Artillery). There they engaged Maj. Gen. William T. Sherman's veterans in the first real combat experience for the gunners, and Stevenson lost thirteen killed. Nevertheless, he won praise for escaping with his wounded despite being enveloped on both flanks. He and the survivors returned to Fort Fisher in time for the attack in January 1865 but not for the bombardment in December 1864. Because Stevenson was absent for the first assault and injured during the second Federal attempt, the responsibility for the companies of the 2d Artillery in Fort Fisher during both engagements rested upon Capt. Daniel Munn of Company B.

Reinforcements raced to Fisher when the Union fleet appeared in December 1864. On December 23, companies F (Walsh's Battery) and K (Washington Grays) of the 1st North Carolina Artillery (10th North Carolina State Troops) came from Smithville with Maj. James Reilly. Ironically, Reilly had been the U.S. Army sergeant who surrendered Fort Johnson at Wilmington to militia in April 1861. Among the militia commanders who then occupied Johnson, where Reilly had been the only soldier, were Stevenson and John J. Hedrick. Of Reilly's companies in 1864, K had surrendered in Fort Hatteras on the North Carolina coast in August 1861, while F was captured at Fort Macon on the North Carolina coast in April 1862.

Both had served at Wilmington and had seen little combat since their exchange.

Other companies sent as reinforcements to Fort Fisher had even less combat experience. Companies E (Scotch Greys) and K (Bladen Artillery Guards) of the 3d North Carolina Artillery (40th North Carolina State Troops) transferred to Fisher from Smith Island. Several companies from the 3d Artillery, including E and K, had served with Hedrick in Fisher until they were sent to Smith Island and formally organized after President Davis's inspection in November 1863. When other companies from the 3d Regiment went to Savannah in December 1864, Companies E and K remained behind. Company D (Rowan Artillery) from the 1st North Carolina Heavy Artillery Battalion

JAMES M. STEVENSON

Born Craven County, North Carolina; commanded Cape Fear Light Artillery during occupation of Union posts at Wilmington in April 1861; became lieutenant of same unit when it mustered as Company C, 2d North Carolina Artillery (36th North Carolina State Troops); during October 1861 became captain of Company A (King Artillery) in same regiment; posted at Fort Caswell near Wilmington until early 1864, when company was transferred to Fort Fisher; elected major of regiment; led five companies to Savannah in November 1864 to oppose advance of Maj. Gen. William T. Sherman; outflanked in sharp fight at Harrison's Old Field; lost thirteen men killed, but brought all of wounded and guns safely back to Savannah; commended by Lt. Gen. William J. Hardee; returned to Fort Fisher and resumed command of 2d North Carolina Artillery despite illness; knocked from parapet and almost paralyzed by shell on January 15, 1865; captured and taken to Fort Columbus at New York City, where he died of pneumonia at the age of thirty-nine on February 18, 1865.

had also earlier worked on Fisher and now returned to the fort from Smithville. Company C (Sutton's Battery) of the 3d North Carolina Light Artillery Battalion had served in Virginia and North Carolina but had never been in combat. Finally, Company D (Kennedy Artillery) of the 13th North Carolina Light Artillery Battalion had campaigned independently and as part of Lamb's 2d North Carolina Artillery before joining the 13th Battalion, but again its men had never endured a battle.

Because so many units were away from Wilmington in December 1864, Lamb had to rely upon four battalions of Junior Reserves, the 1st, 4th, 7th, and 8th. These units were organized after the draft was extended in February 1864 to include males who were seventeen years of age as reserves. The youths who served at Fort Fisher were from all over North Carolina. The 1st came from Asheboro, the 4th from Raleigh, the 7th from Wilmington, and the 8th from Morganton (despite a Federal raid that captured more than a hundred young recruits). By the time they arrived at Fisher, these youths had already become veterans, having campaigned in bitter cold at Belfield, Virginia, in December 1864. There they had earned a commendation from the North Carolina legislature for their role in a futile effort to block a Federal attack on the Weldon Railroad at that point.

Fisher's gun crews were supplemented by sailors and marines from Battery Buchanan, where they served under Capt. Robert T. Chapman. Most of the navy men came from the CSS *Chickamauga*. Led by Lt. Francis M. Roby, a detachment raced to Fort Fisher on Christmas Day, 1864, to crew two Brooke rifled guns taken from a sunken gunboat and installed on the seaface. Lamb had no one experienced with such weapons before the *Chickamauga* crewmen, whose vessel had several Brooke rifles, arrived. More sailors and the marines came later that day under the command of Capt. Alfred C. Van Benthuysen, a New York adventurer who fought in China and Italy before the war. He had been court-martialed several times for insubordinate behavior, but he and his marines would be commended by Whiting for their work at Fisher in December 1864.

Conspicuous by their exclusion from the grateful resolution of the Confederate Congress were Bragg, Maj. Gen. Robert F. Hoke, and the men of the latter's division. Bragg was commonly blamed for the loss of Fort Fisher, which seemed proper in light of his disappointing career elsewhere in the Confederacy. A former U.S. Army officer, he had begun the war with great promise, having fought the Seminoles and won three brevets during the Mexican War. Although retired from the army since 1856, he was

BRAXTON BRAGG

Born North Carolina 1817; graduated U.S. Military Academy fifth in the 1837 class of fifty; appointed 2d lieutenant 3rd Artillery; promoted to 1st lieutenant in 1838 and to captain in 1846; participated in the Seminole War and won three brevet promotions for gallant conduct during the Mexican War; in 1849 married Eliza Brooks Ellis, daughter of a Louisiana sugar cane planter; after routine garrison duty on the frontier, he resigned his brevet lieutenant colonelcy in 1856 to become a Louisiana sugar planter; in 1861 appointed Confederate brigadier general and assigned to Pensacola, Florida, where he changed the volunteers he found there into drilled and disciplined soldiers; promoted to major general and assigned command of the Gulf Coast from Pensacola to Mobile; in 1862 he received orders to move his troops by rail to join General A. S. Johnston's army at Corinth, Mississippi, for the Battle of Shiloh, during which Bragg served as army chief of staff and commanded a corps; after Johnston's death, upon the recommendation of his successor, General P.G.T. Beauregard, Bragg was promoted to full general; in June he in turn replaced General Beauregard when that officer took an unauthorized sick leave; deciding to invade Kentucky, Bragg moved the bulk of his army from Tupelo, Mississippi, to Chattanooga, Tennessee, by rail, and then joined General E. Kirby Smith in a appointed a brigadier general in 1861 and rose to full general within a year. Bragg's retreat from Kentucky in 1862, followed by the loss of Chattanooga in 1863, had led to his removal from active command and assignment as chief of staff for Jefferson Davis, who was apparently still very fond of him. When an attack seemed eminent at Wilmington, Bragg was assigned as the local department commander, prompting a Richmond newspaper editor to lament, in bold type, "Goodbye Wilmington!"

bold invasion of Kentucky; checked at Perryville in October by General D.C. Buell, Bragg retreated to Murfreesboro, Tennessee, where he fought a bloody battle against General W.S. Rosecrans in late 1862 and early 1863; Rosecrans's Tullahoma Campaign in June 1863 compelled Bragg to abandon Tennessee, but after receiving General James Longstreet's Corps from Virginia in September as reinforcements for the Battle of Chickamauga, he drove the Federals back into Chattanooga and began a siege that lasted until General U.S. Grant arrived from Mississippi in November 1863 and drove the Confederates back into Georgia; relieved of command of the Army of Tennessee, Bragg became President Davis's military adviser in February 1864; he exercised considerable power and served the president and the Confederacy well during the eight months he held this position, but his appointment came too late in the war for him to have a determinative impact; in January 1865, while still serving as the president's military adviser, Bragg engaged in his most ineffective performance as a field commander: he failed to prevent the Federals from taking Fort Fisher, which protected Wilmington, North Carolina, the last Confederate port open to blockade runners; Bragg spent the last weeks of the war under the command of General J.E. Johnston attempting to check General W.T. Sherman's advance; Bragg and his wife were part of the Confederate flight from Richmond until their capture in Georgia; Bragg, who lived in relative poverty after the war, died in Galveston, Texas, in 1876, and is buried in Mobile. Never a great field commander, he had talents the Confederacy needed but seldom used: the army possessed no better disciplinarian or drillmaster; an able organizer and administrator, he excelled as an inspector, possessed a good eye for strategy, and proved himself a dedicated patriot.

Bragg returned to Wilmington from Savannah on December 17, 1864, without many of the troops he had taken with him. This convinced Gen. Robert E. Lee to detach Hoke's division from the Army of Northern Virginia and send it to Wilmington. Hoke was a North Carolinian who had served with distinction in all of Lee's campaigns, then earned a promotion to major general by capturing the port of Plymouth in his home state in April 1864. His troops were combat veterans, but only a portion of a North Carolina brigade, commanded by Brig. Gen. William W. Kirkland, arrived for the December 1864 engagement. Kirkland, a former U.S. Marine who had attended West Point without graduating, had inherited his men in August 1864 after recovering from his third wound. They had originally marched to Virginia in May 1864 under the command of Brig. Gen. James G. Martin. He left after his health failed, but the troops stayed and fought in the bitter clashes around Petersburg until ordered home with Kirkland in December 1864.

Two regiments of Kirkland's brigade, the 17th and 42d North Carolina Infantry, arrived at Sugar Loaf near Fort Fisher at about the same time as the Federal fleet in December 1864, and a hundred men of the 66th North Carolina Infantry came later. They were aided during the ensuing operation by the 2d South Carolina Cavalry, veterans of hard campaigns in Virginia like Kirkland's troops, as well as Company I (Wilmington Horse Artillery) of the 1st North Carolina Artillery, the 8th North Carolina Senior Reserves, and the 7th North Carolina Home Guards. Both the Reserves and Home Guards were men too old or infirm for extended service. The former, led by Allmand A. McKoy, were organized with the 4th, 7th, and 8th Junior Reserve Battalions as a brigade under the command of John K. Connally, who had lost his left arm at Gettysburg as colonel of the 55th North Carolina Infantry. Col. James G. Burr led the Home Guards. One of Kirkland's officers recalled the sad sight of gray-haired men lying dead or wounded at Sugar Loaf. In January 1865 the Home Guards replaced the Junior Reserves in Connally's brigade, which was then posted closer to Wilmington, but some sources report that two Home Guard companies served at Fisher during the final engagement on January 15, 1865.

Lamb's garrison received a welcome permanent addition after the Federals left in December 1864 and most of the emergency reinforcements returned to their usual posts of duty. Companies E and K of the 3d North Carolina Artillery transferred to Fort Fisher from Smith Island. In fact, Company E had originally mustered as Company D of the 2d Artillery, under Lamb's command, before changing its assignment. Settled once more at Fisher, they returned to the labor of readying the post for an attack. When the Federal fleet reappeared in mid-January 1865, the ten companies of the 2d Artillery and the two from the 3d Artillery composed the permanent garrison of Fort Fisher.

As the Federals invested Fisher in January 1865, once more other units hustled to the fort. Companies F and K of the 1st Regiment returned, while Company I of the same regiment stayed at Sugar Loaf with Hoke. Company D of the 1st Battalion again came from Fort Caswell, along with Company C of the 3d North Carolina Light Artillery Battalion. Two additional companies of the 3d Artillery Regiment, D (Gatlin Artillery) and G (Herring Artillery), arrived from Smith Island. D and G had been among the five companies of their regiment ordered to Savannah. They, like their comrades from the 2d North Carolina Artillery, narrowly escaped disaster when Federals enveloped them. That was not the first debacle for Company G; it was driven from the field at New Bern in March 1862. Company G had also previously served in Lamb's regiment until it transferred, like several other artillery companies at Fisher in January 1865. The last artillery unit to enter the fort was Company D of the 13th North Carolina Light Artillery Battalion. Finally, dozens of seamen and marines, including Van Benthuysen, came for the final fight.

All of Hoke's veterans were present in January. Along with Kirkland's men, another brigade of North Carolinians, nominally led by Brig. Gen. Thomas L. Clingman, also returned to its home state after hard combat in Virginia. These men had fought under the direction of Clingman at Goldsboro in 1862 and Battery Wagner at Charleston in 1863, as well as in Virginia, but he did not lead them at Fort Fisher. The general had gone home after being wounded in August 1864, leaving his troops to Col. Hector M. McKethan of the 51st North Carolina Infantry. Hoke's two other brigades were from Georgia and South Carolina, led respectively by brigadier generals Alfred H. Colquitt and Johnson Hagood. Colquitt, like Hoke, had earned distinction under Lee and came south earlier to combat a Union incursion: he defeated the Federals at Olustee, Florida, in February 1864. Returning to Petersburg, he fought alongside Hagood's troops who, like those in Clingman's brigade, had fought at Battery Wagner before going to Virginia to block Lt. Gen. Ulysses S. Grant's drive toward Richmond in May 1864. Hagood was on leave while his brigade was at Fisher, so his men were under the temporary command of Col. Robert F. Graham of the 21st South Carolina Infantry.

Hoke's division was supported by a host of other units at Sugar Loaf in January 1865, as it had been just a month earlier. The 2d South Carolina Cavalry remained, as did Company I of the 1st North Carolina Artillery. They were joined by Company A (Northampton Artillery) of the 3d North Carolina Light Artillery Battalion, which endured garrison duty for most of the war, and by the Staunton Hill Artillery, a Virginia unit that spent most of the war guarding salt works near Wilmington. The enhanced Confederate artillery force at Sugar Loaf was intended to make it more difficult for Union troops to land and to bolster an attack on any invaders who made it ashore.

The first Federal commander to try the garrison of Fort Fisher and its supporting troops was Maj. Gen. Benjamin F. Butler. As commander of the Department of Virginia and North Carolina, he superseded the officer chosen by Grant to command the expedition, Maj. Gen. Godfrey Weitzel. The older Butler officially declared that Weitzel, who was twenty-nine years of age, was too young and inexperienced to handle such an operation. In fact, Butler was hoping to regain some of the fame he had lost. He had begun well by capturing the Confederate posts at Cape Hatteras in 1861 but became notorious for his actions later at New Orleans. There he had a man hanged for tearing down a U.S. flag, declared that any woman who was disrespectful to a Federal officer would be jailed as a prostitute, and allegedly stole private property. Ordered to Bermuda Hundred for an attack on Petersburg in May 1864, he floundered and accomplished nothing while Grant pushed his own troops forward in a grueling drive for Richmond.

Weitzel, who remained second in command for the expedition, led fragments of two new corps into combat at Fisher, though he was familiar with a large portion of them. He had begun the war as only a lieutenant but had commanded troops under Butler in Louisiana and had been promoted rapidly. He enjoyed the full confidence of Butler, despite the latter's self-serving comments about his youth and lack of experience. Until December 3, 1864, Weitzel led the XVIII Corps, but as of that date his white troops were sent to the new XXIV Corps while his black units were reassigned to the new XXV Corps, to which he was then assigned as commander. Thus, brigades from his old corps, serving with either Brig. Gen. Adelbert Ames's Second Division of the XXIV Corps or Brig. Gen. Charles J. Paine's Third Division of the XXV Corps, primarily composed Butler's land forces at Fort Fisher.

The white troops of Ames's division were mostly veterans of operations in Virginia and along the Atlantic coast, as were the officers. The combative and ambitious Ames graduated from West Point ten weeks before he was wounded at First Bull Run, where he earned a Medal of Honor. He recovered and fought in almost every major battle in the East, rising to the rank of brigadier general and winning a string of commendations. Newton M. Curtis had also been wounded, in 1862, but spent much of the ensuing time at a desk. Nevertheless, he led the First Brigade of Ames's division as a colonel with a brevet to brigadier general. The leader of the Second Brigade of Ames's division, Col. Galusha Pennypacker, was the youngest brigade commander in the army at twenty years of age. Though not yet old enough to vote, he already had been wounded thirteen times. Col. Louis Bell, the son of a New Hampshire governor and senator, led the Third Brigade of

Ames's division. A lawyer before the war, he like his fellow officers had been wounded in combat while rising through the ranks to command.

Curtis's brigade comprised New York infantry entirely: the 3d, 112th (Chautauqua Regiment), 117th (4th Oneida

BENJAMIN F. BUTLER

Born Deerfield, New Hampshire, November 5, 1818; moved to Lowell, Massachusetts, where his mother operated a boarding house after his father died; graduated from Waterville College (nee Colby University) in Maine, 1838; admitted to the bar in Lowell, 1840, and focused on criminal law; elected as Democrat to Massachusetts House of Representatives, 1853; elected to state senate, 1859; attended Democratic national convention at Charleston, 1860, and supported Jefferson Davis as candidate for president; attended Baltimore convention that same year and endorsed John C. Breckinridge for president; entered military service as brigadier general of Massachusetts militia; broke blockade of Washington and was first to be appointed major general of volunteers by Abraham Lincoln; defeated at Big Bethel, June 1861; captured Hatteras Inlet, August 1861; occupied New Orleans, April 1862; conduct as military governor led to controversy and his removal in December 1862; given command of Army of the James; trapped in Bermuda Hundred during advance on Petersburg, May 1864; served as overall commander of expedition to Fort Fisher, December 1864; returned to Massachusetts, January 1865; resigned from army, November 1865; elected as a Republican to the U.S. House of Representatives, 1866, and remained until 1875; manager in impeachment of Andrew Johnson; elected to Congress as candidate for Greenback Party, 1876, and served one term; elected governor of Massachusetts, 1882; Greenback Party candidate for president, 1884; died at Washington on January 11, 1893 and buried in Lowell.

Regiment), and 142d Regiments. Of these units, the 3d New York Infantry had the longest history, having fought at Big Bethel, Virginia, the first major engagement of the war, in June 1861. Ironically, the Federals there had been repulsed by North Carolina troops. The four regiments of Curtis's brigade first worked together in the siege of Suffolk during April and May of 1862, then traveled to Charleston in the summer of 1863 to participate in the siege and capture of Battery Wagner. They were also heavily engaged in Butler's clumsy Bermuda Hundred campaign, then fought in many of the bloody engagements before Petersburg in the summer of 1864

NEWTON M. CURTIS

Born New York 1835; worked as teacher, farmer, and postmaster before war; captain of Company G, 16th New York Infantry until May 1862, when he was badly wounded on the Peninsula; assigned to administrative duties; returned to field as brevet brigadier general in command of First Brigade, Second Division, XXIV Corps in summer of 1864 at Petersburg; disappointed with cancellation of planned assault at Fort Fisher in December 1864; feuded bitterly with division commander, Brig. Gen. Adelbert Ames; led the attack on Shepherd's Battery at Fort Fisher in January 1865 with his First Brigade; defied order from Ames and continued advance until he was struck in face by shell fragment, losing left eye and part of facial bone; dragged from parapet by troops who assumed he was dead; doctor ordered coffin, but Curtis survived a long recovery; awarded Medal of Honor; promoted to brigadier general and brevetted major general; returned to New York, became collector of

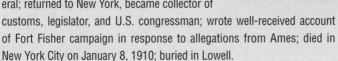

customs, legislator, and U.S. congressman; wrote well-received account of Fort Fisher campaign in response to allegations from Ames; died in New York City on January 8, 1910; buried in Lowell.

under the direction of Curtis, who returned to the field during that time.

Pennypacker's brigade was a mix of New York and Pennsylvania regiments. The 47th (Washington Grays) and 48th (Continental Guard) regiments of New York infantry had worked together in the capture of Port Royal, South Carolina, in the fall of 1861, the reduction of Fort Pulaski during the spring of 1862, the siege and capture of Battery Wagner in the summer of 1863, the battle of Olustee in February 1864, and in Butler's operations around Petersburg in the summer of 1864. Two of the three Pennsylvania regiments, the 76th (Keystone Zouaves) and 97th, had also served in the Port Royal and Battery Wagner campaigns as well as during other operations along the Atlantic coast and in Virginia under the command of Butler. The 203d Pennsylvania Infantry, however, was relatively new. They had mustered during September 1864 and since that time had served in the investment of Richmond, taking part in a pitched battle only once, at Fair Oaks in late October.

Bell's brigade included two New York infantry regiments, the 115th (Iron Hearted Regiment) and 169th (Troy Regiment), as well as infantry regiments from Indiana, the 13th, and New Hampshire, the 4th. The 115th New York was among the troops who surrendered at Harpers Ferry to Maj. Gen. Thomas J. "Stonewall" Jackson in September 1862. The 169th New York had participated in the sieges of Suffolk and Battery Wagner before joining Butler in Virginia. The 13th Indiana had begun its service in West Virginia during 1861, then fought in the Shenandoah Valley against Jackson before participating in the sieges of Suffolk and Battery Wagner as well as the fighting at Petersburg in 1864. The 4th New Hampshire had the most experience in fighting along the coast, having taken part in the capture of Port Royal and in operations elsewhere in South Carolina, including Battery Wagner, and Florida for three years. They too had joined Butler in Virginia for the summer campaigns of 1864.

Paine's Third Division served in the XXV Corps, the only black corps ever created. Paine was a Harvard-educated attorney and the great-grandson of a signer of the Declaration of Independence. At Fisher he had two infantry brigades led by Colonels John W. Ames, a lieutenant in the prewar army, and Elias Wright, who began the war as a lieutenant in a New Jersey regiment. The former commanded the 4th, 6th, 30th, and 39th U.S. Colored Troops. The 4th and 6th had mustered in Maryland and Pennsylvania respectively. They endured garri-

ALFRED H. TERRY

Born November 10, 1827, Hartford, Connecticut; attended Yale Law School but withdrew after being admitted to the bar in 1849; clerk of New Haven County Superior Court, 1854-60; entered military service as colonel of 2d Connecticut Infantry, a ninety-day militia unit that he commanded at Bull Run, July 1861; recruited 7th Connecticut Infantry and led them in capture of Port Royal, November 1861, and Fort Pulaski, April 1862; appointed brigadier general of volunteers, April 1862; participated in battles of Secessionville and Battery Wagner during siege of Charleston; joined Army of the James as commander of X Corps, 1863; participated in Bermuda Hundred and Petersburg operations; accompanied Federal expedition to Fort Fisher, December 1864; commanded second expedition to Fisher, which fell one day before he became a major general of volunteers; received thanks of Congress and commission as brigadier general in U.S. Army for the victo-ry; attached with X Corps to Army of the Ohio for operations in North Carolina; remained in army after the war and served in west; commanded Department of Dakota and personally directed field operations that included Battle of Little Bighorn, 1876; made major general of U.S. Army, 1886 (the first Civil War volunteer officer to make that grade and one of only three in the service at that time); retired, 1888; died December 16, 1890, at New Haven, Connecticut, where he was buried.

son duty at Yorktown, Virginia, from the summer of 1863 until they became involved in Butler's effort to take Petersburg during May 1864 and the ensuing siege. The 30th and 39th were newer, having mustered at Baltimore just a few months before marching to Butler in Virginia. Wright had the 1st, 5th, 10th, 37th, and 107th U.S. Colored Troops. The 1st organized in the District of Columbia, then joined the 5th, from Ohio, on the Virginia coast in the summer of 1863. There the 10th mustered during the late fall of that same year. These three units joined Butler in May 1864, and subsequently two new regiments, the 107th and 37th, came. The 107th, from Kentucky, served little more than a month in Virginia before embarking for Fort Fisher; ironically, the 37th had been recruited in North Carolina.

Butler did not bring much artillery with him in December, preferring to rely upon the navy to reduce Fisher. He had just two batteries, the 16th New York Light Battery (Dickinson Light Artillery) and Battery E of the 3d U.S. Artillery. The former had served for a year in the defenses of Washington, then participated in the siege of Suffolk and campaigned with Butler in Virginia in 1864. The men of Battery E were seasoned veterans by the time they came to North Carolina. They had fought at Bull Run and Port Royal in 1861, in South Carolina and Florida in 1862, at Battery Wagner in 1863, and at Olustee and Petersburg in 1864.

For the second Federal effort in January 1865, Grant chose a new commander, Alfred H. Terry, and provided more troops. A Yale alumnus who worked before the war as the clerk of court at New Haven, Connecticut, Terry had done well at Port Royal, Fort Pulaski, and Battery Wagner and rose in rank from colonel to brevet major general. He made two changes in Butler's order of battle. The 27th U.S. Colored Troops, Petersburg veterans from Ohio, replaced the 107th in Wright's brigade, while Ames's division was augmented by the addition of Col. Joseph C. Abbott's Second Brigade of the First Division. Abbott before the war was a newspaper editor, but he had enlisted as the lieutenant colonel of the 7th New Hampshire Infantry, which remained in his brigade. Of all those who came south to attack Fort Fisher, he apparently was the most impressed with Wilmington. He returned to the port city after the war and published a newspaper there until his death in 1881, despite the enmity of many locals for transplanted Northerners.

Abbott's brigade, which had formerly been led by Terry, included two regiments of Connecticut infantry, the 6th and 7th (Terry's original regiment), and two of New Hampshire infantry, the 3d and 7th. The first pair were veterans of hard fighting at Port Royal, Fort Pulaski, and Battery Wagner before joining the forces commanded by Butler at Petersburg. In addition, the 7th Connecticut fought at Olustee in 1864. The 3d New Hampshire served at Port Royal during 1861, when the 7th regiment of New Hampshire infantry was baking in the heat of Dry Tortugas. The 3d stayed in South Carolina and fought at Battery Wagner, then traveled to Florida before being assigned to Butler in May 1864 in Virginia. The 7th New Hampshire shuttled between Florida and South Carolina during the same period, fighting at Battery Wagner and Olustee, before joining Butler as well in May 1864.

Told by Grant to begin a siege if his assault was repulsed, Terry also brought an engineering detachment and more artillery batteries. The engineers were Companies A, B, and H of the 15th New York Engineers. The first two had begun the war as infantry. Reorganized, they served on the Peninsula, in Maryland, and at Fredericksburg during 1862; at Chancellorsville and Gettysburg in 1863; and with the Army of the Potomac again as it marched into Virginia in 1864, fighting in the Wilderness and before Richmond. The regiment was completed with the addition of seven companies in November 1864; among these was Company H. The new artillery comprised Batteries B, G, and L of the 1st Connecticut Heavy Artillery and a portion of the 16th New York Heavy Artillery (Companies A, B, C, F, G, and K). The Connecticut gunners had begun the war as infantry but reorganized for the Peninsula campaign in 1862. Since that time, they had served in the Washington garrison, though Company B was sent to fight at Fredericksburg, Chancellorsville, and Gettysburg. The New

York artillery companies had mustered in sequence from September through January 1864 and first experienced combat in the lines at Petersburg.

Terry found that the line he had chosen to defend against a possible counterattack by Hoke was longer than expected, so he accepted a proposal for the addition of a naval detachment to his assaulting force. No fewer than 1,861 volunteers from the Union fleet, representing almost every warship in the flotilla, were put ashore with pistols and cutlasses on January 15 to attack the fort. Accompanying them were 400 marines, some of whom carried carbines. The entire assembly was under the direction of Lt. Comdr. K. Randolph Breese, who also was the captain of the Federal fleet. Thirty-three years of age, Breese had been at sea since he was only fifteen, serving under Capt. David G. Farragut during the Mexican War and accompanying Commodore Matthew Perry on his trip to Japan in 1853.

Breese had commanded the mortar fleet with Farragut's foster brother, Rear Adm. David D. Porter, at New Orleans and Vicksburg, and again served under Porter at Fisher during December 1864 and January 1865. Porter came from four generations of sailors. Now at the age of fifty-one, he had served for almost four decades with the U.S. Navy, having begun as a midshipman at the age of thirteen. He served with distinction during the Mexican War and won fame for his victory at New Orleans in 1862 and his successful operations with the Mississippi Squadron at Vicksburg. The Fisher campaign provided a chance to regain some of his reputation, which had been somewhat tarnished by the disastrous Red River campaign in the spring of 1864.

Porter gathered a variety of warships to pound Fort Fisher into submission. Sixty-one armed vessels with 635 guns took part in the bombardment of Fisher in December 1864. After Porter reorganized his fleet for the January 1865 attack, he had sixty ships with a total armament of 611 guns. This flotilla included three ironclad single-turret monitors, one double-turret monitor (*Monadnock*), gunboats propelled by either side wheels or screw propellers, and wooden-hulled steam frigates.

Porter's largest steam frigate was the *Colorado,* with fifty guns, followed by the *Minnesota* and *Wabash,* with forty-six and forty-four respectively. Any one of these three vessels had enough guns to match or outdo Fisher. The pride of Porter's fleet was the *New Ironsides,* whose hull was sheathed with

DAVID DIXON PORTER

Born Pennsylvania 1813; son of Commodore David Porter, he accompanied his father's pirate suppression expeditions in the Gulf of Mexico; having spent much of his early life at sea, he received little formal education; joined the Mexican Navy as a midshipman in 1827, joined U.S. Navy as midshipman in 1829; lieutenant 1841; saw considerable service during the Mexican War; served various merchant enterprises but returned to active duty in 1855; with the outbreak of Civil War, served in blockade squadrons; promoted to commander in 1861 after twenty years as a lieutenant; capably led the mortar flotilla in the capture of New Orleans; given command of the Mississippi Squadron in October 1862; for his excellent service during the Vicksburg Campaign he was elevated to rear admiral, bypassing the ranks of captain and commodore; took a large fleet up the Red River to support Major General Nathaniel P. Banks' ill-fated campaign; the fleet was harassed by Confederate land forces and slowed by low water levels during its difficult

retreat; sent East, he directed the North Atlantic Squadron for the balance of the war, participating in the capture of Fort Fisher, North Carolina; superintendent of the United States Naval Academy, 1865-1869; vice admiral 1866; admiral 1870; author of numerous books including *Incidents of the Civil War* (1886) and *History of the Navy During the War of the Rebellion* (1890); he died 1891. The failure of the Red River Expedition notwithstanding, Admiral Porter played a significant role in the Federal success in the West. He was the cousin of Major General Fitz-John Porter.

four inches of iron. This warship carried fourteen 11-inch
guns, two 150-pounders, and two 60-pounders. The equally
durable but more lightly armed *Monadnock* boasted four 15-
inch guns whose shells weighed three hundred pounds each.
Ironically, the *Malvern,* Porter's flagship from which he directed the greatest naval bombardment in the war, was a former
blockade runner, the *Ella and Annie.* This side-wheeler had
been captured at Wilmington in November 1863.

USS *WABASH*

Wooden-hulled screw frigate launched at Philadelphia Navy Yard in
October 1855; served as flagship in effort to foil William Walker's invasion
of Nicaragua in 1857; participated in Federal occupation of Hatteras Inlet,
North Carolina, in
August 1861; served as
flagship in capture of
Port Royal, South
Carolina, in November
1861; assigned to block-
ade of Charleston and
proved effective despite
top speed of only nine
knots per hour; target of
unsuccessful attack by a
Confederate *David,* a
semisubmerged torpedo
boat, in April 1864; under command of Capt. Melancton Smith, took part
in bombardment of Fort Fisher in December 1864 and January 1865 as
part of Rear Adm. David D. Porter's second line of battle; fired hundreds
of shells from batteries that included 9- and 10-inch Dahlgren smooth-
bores and rifled Parrott guns; decommissioned at Boston Navy Yard on
February 14, 1865; returned to service in October 1871 and became flagship for Rear Adm. James Alden, a naval veteran of the Fort Fisher
attacks, who commanded the Mediterranean Squadron; decommissioned
for last time in April 1874 at Boston Navy Yard; used as receiving ship
until 1912, when it was sold for scrap.

Porter's fleet greatly outnumbered the Confederate ships at Wilmington. Two ironclads had been completed at the city in 1864 but were no longer afloat by December. The *North Carolina* had weak engines and had served as a floating battery until it sank at Smithville (Southport); worms had eaten its wooden hull. The *Raleigh* made one sortie on May 6, fired a handful of shots at the blockaders (one of which fell inside Fort Fisher), then withdrew into the Cape Fear River, where it ran aground; tides broke the ship apart. There was a third ironclad under construction at Wilmington, but it was burned in the shipyard when the city fell in early 1865. The failure of the ironclads left only a few transports and armed vessels to the Southern defenders. The best was the *Chickamauga*, a steamer with three guns that had been a commerce raider, but there was also the *Arctic*, a three-gun floating battery, and the *Yadkin*, a converted tugboat with one gun. The *Chickamauga* shelled the Union troops as they advanced in January 1865, but the tiny gunboat was driven away by artillery fire.

With no significant Confederate fleet, the outnumbered and outgunned Confederates in Fort Fisher were left on their own in January 1865 to face an overwhelming naval bombardment and a determined assault by Terry's blue-clad veterans. Prior to that, however, they would acquit themselves well against a much more timid foe, Butler, whose hesitation puzzled both his own naval commander, Porter, and the Confederate officers in charge at Fort Fisher, Lamb and Whiting. Butler's failure in December 1864 would cheat his men of the glory they eagerly expected, but most of them would get a second chance at the garrison of Fisher less than one month later, when both sides, victor and vanquished, would earn national respect for their hard fighting.

4

SUCH A RAIN

FIRST ASSAULT ON FORT FISHER, DECEMBER 24–27, 1864

Peter W. Alexander, a newspaper reporter flamboyantly advertised as the "Prince of Correspondents" by one of his employers, was in Wilmington when Fort Fisher was bombarded on Christmas Eve, 1864. Although he was not usually prone to use melodramatic prose, he wrote that "such a rain of shot and shell never before fell upon any spot of earth since gunpowder was invented." A few days later, he reported that Maj. Gen. Benjamin F. Butler's attack had failed, which led Alexander to conclude that Fort Fisher was "the strongest earthwork in the world." While Fisher may not have deserved such an accolade, it certainly proved to be more than Butler could handle.

The Union capture of the forts at the mouth of Mobile Bay in August 1864 effectively closed that port for the

Confederacy, and the attention of the Federals focused on the only major harbor still available to blockade runners in the eastern Confederacy: Wilmington. That city by late 1864 was the port of choice for four out of five blockade runners bound for the Carolinas, and almost six times as many runners departed from Wilmington as from Charleston in 1864. At the same time, Wilmington greatly overshadowed any port outside of that region. This increasing activity attracted the notice of Secretary of the Navy Gideon Welles and his staff, and they consulted with Pres. Abraham Lincoln about a combined operation to close Wilmington. The idea seemed timely, but the final decision was left to Lt. Gen. Ulysses S. Grant as the general in chief.

Grant approved the idea, but troops would have to come from Butler, who was accomplishing nothing in Bermuda Hundred, and not the embattled Army of the Potomac, which was locked in a death struggle with Gen. Robert E. Lee's Army of Northern Virginia at Petersburg. As commander of the operation, Grant chose Maj. Gen. Godfrey Weitzel of the XXV Corps. He was to cooperate with Rear Adm. David D. Porter, who with Grant's approval was given command of the Union fleet assigned to attack Fort Fisher. Unfortunately for the potential success of Grant's plans, at the last moment Weitzel's superior, Butler, announced that he would accompany the Fisher expedition as overall commander. Butler and Porter had been feuding ever since the capture of New Orleans in 1862, when the admiral accepted the surrender of the forts below the city before the general could arrive and do so. They would fail again to work effectively as partners at Fort Fisher.

Porter's fleet of sixty-one warships, escorting dozens of transports carrying Butler's 6,500 troops, assembled at Hampton Roads. They sailed on December 13, 1864. Storms scattered the vessels, but finally most arrived at the chosen rendezvous point near Fort Fisher on the evening of December 18. The next day, organized into three battle lines, the fleet steamed within sight of Fisher. The arrival of the Federal ships suddenly ended the ongoing construction at Fort Fisher, and Col. William Lamb sent his gangs of slaves to Wilmington for safety. The garrison left their huts and tents in camps outside of Fisher and took their stations inside the post. Meanwhile, Lamb's wife and their two children evacuated to a home on the far side of the Cape Fear River; they would watch the fighting from there through binoculars.

A storm forced the Federal transports to seek shelter at Beaufort, a Union-occupied port up the coast from Fort Fisher, and Porter began his attack before Butler could return. During the night of December 23, an iron-hulled Union steamer, the USS *Louisiana,* packed with 215 tons of black powder was exploded near the earthwork. The scheme was the brainchild of Butler, who got the notion from reports of a powder magazine exploding near London, England. Allegedly, houses were flattened and windows shattered for a twenty-mile radius when the magazine had erupted. Porter had been skeptical at first, but Butler convinced him that it would work despite reports to the contrary from more qualified military experts. Grant never did believe it would succeed.

The captain of the powder ship was Comdr. Alexander C. Rhind. The doomed vessel was disguised as a blockade runner by adding a fake smokestack, painting it a dull gray, and further modifying its lines. The USS *Wilderness* towed the floating bomb close to Fisher, then cast it loose in the darkness and waited nearby to pick up its crew. Just after Rhind started his engines, he spied the *Little Hattie,* a blockade runner, and cleverly decided to follow it closer to shore. He slipped within 600 yards of Fisher and, along with his second in command, Samuel W. Preston, and a volunteer, he stayed behind as the rest of the crew left the powder ship. They set the detonators, but Rhind also lit a slow fire in the stern. This proved to be a good decision; the fire actually ignited part of the powder more than two hours after Rhind left the ship—the detonators apparently failed completely.

The explosion came about 1:30 A.M. on December 24. It awakened some Confederate sailors who had been sent to Fort Fisher to man a battery of two Brooke rifles. They ran out to watch the ship self-destruct and then returned to their beds, quite unimpressed with the spectacle. The Federals all agreed that the effort was a flop; Rhind, who watched from a safe distance, said bitterly, "There's a fizzle." The effort failed because the ship carried much less powder than the 300 tons requested by Butler. Too, the load was so heavy that a layer of explosive shells and additional incendiary devices was not put aboard the ship, which almost foundered with the lethal cargo that it did carry. Some also argued that if the charges had detonated all at once, the effect would have been greatly enhanced. This may not have been of much importance, for the ship exploded much farther than the 450 yards from the work recommended by those navy experts who did endorse the plan. The vessel drifted after Rhind left it, igniting at a distance of at least 1,100 yards.

There were many causes for the failure of Butler's powder boat, but one effect was clear: Fort Fisher was unscathed by the blast and would have to be reduced by a naval bombardment. On December 24 the Union fleet pounded the garrison for five hours, firing more than 10,000 rounds from 635 guns. Lamb's forty-four siege guns, mounted on the platforms along the landface and seaface of Fort Fisher, fired just 672 times in response. The USS *New Ironsides* hurled the first shot for the Federals from one of its 11-inch guns. At Lamb's signal the Confederates responded with a shot from the 10-inch smoothbore Columbiad on the Northeast Bastion, which tore a hole through the stack of the USS *Susquehanna*. Lamb did not allow a heavy return fire because he had only 3,600 rounds for his artillery. For his Armstrong rifled gun, the pride of Lamb's batteries, he had just thirteen 150-pound shells, and its crew was forbidden to fire at all unless he gave them a direct order.

Maj. Gen. William H.C. Whiting arrived about four hours after the bombardment began, walking across the sand from Battery Buchanan with three aides through a rain of shells. When the Union fleet appeared, he had tried to commandeer several blockade runners to serve as obstacles to an anticipated Federal run through New Inlet, but department commander Gen. Braxton Bragg refused to allow such a confiscation. Whiting then asked naval authorities for the CSS *Chickamauga* and the CSS *Arctic* to block New Inlet, but they refused also.

He finally secured two blockade runners to serve with the CSS *Cape Fear*, an unarmed steamer, as troop transports on the river behind Fisher.

Whiting's first concern was to reinforce Lamb's garrison, which consisted of only five companies of the 2d North Carolina Artillery when the Federals arrived. The general brought with him Maj. James Reilly and two companies, E and K, from the 3d North Carolina Artillery. Capt. James L. McCormic's Company D of the 1st North Carolina Heavy Artillery Battalion also landed at Battery Buchanan and tried to cross the sand to Fort Fisher on December 24, but the Federal fire proved to be too heavy, and they took refuge behind a sandbank. After nightfall, these Confederates made their way into Fisher. They served at gun positions along the seaface, then rushed to the landface and finally to Buchanan with Reilly's troops to meet anticipated Union attacks that never came. Lamb assigned four other companies to a similar sequence of posts as they arrived. Lt. Francis M. Roby led twenty-nine marines and sailors to Fisher, where they crewed the Brooke rifled guns until both pieces burst. Late on Christmas Day, when an assault seemed likely, two-thirds of the naval detachment still at Buchanan under the command of Capt. Robert T. Chapman, perhaps 120 men, hustled to Fort Fisher. All were welcome, but Capt. Alfred C. Van Benthuysen and his marines were singled out for a warm commendation from Whiting.

The general also told Lamb that at least a portion of Maj. Gen. Robert F. Hoke's division, which had been sent from Richmond when an attack on Fort Fisher seemed eminent, had arrived nearby. Two regiments from Brig. Gen. William W. Kirkland's brigade, the 17th and 42d North Carolina Infantry, were at Sugar Loaf as well as part of a third, the 66th North Carolina Infantry. There they were supported by the 2d South Carolina Cavalry, Company I of the 1st North Carolina Artillery, the 8th North Carolina Senior Reserves, and the 7th North Carolina Home Guards. Kirkland also found four battalions of Junior Reserves at Sugar Loaf, but he was ordered to send them to Battery Buchanan. They were to go to Smith Island to replace units that had been sent to Fisher by Col.

John J. Hedrick. Upon their arrival at Buchanan, they found that there were no boats, so Lamb ordered them into the fort on December 25. Their commanders led them across the sand under fire. As they filed into the work, Whiting allegedly told a comrade, "These are North Carolina's pets." Quickly, a young wag in the ranks retorted that his state had a "damned bad way" of showing affection. The 1st and 7th Battalions found shelter in the fort and won the praise of Lamb, but the 4th and 8th Battalions were led by Maj. John M. Reece to works about three miles from Fisher.

While Whiting was shuffling troops, the Union bombardment on December 24 spluttered to a disappointing end for the attackers. They accurately judged that they had scarcely affected the fort or its defenders. Half of the garrison's quarters burned and Lamb's brick headquarters building was pounded to rubble, but little other structural damage was done. A caisson had exploded and an 8-inch smoothbore Columbiad had dismounted itself, but otherwise the fort's armament remained largely intact. Lamb kept his gunners in the bombproofs as much as possible, so he only lost twenty-three men wounded, one mortally, on December 24. One Confederate was especially lucky. Pvt. Christopher Bland from the 2d North Carolina Artillery earned a measure of immortality by twice climbing the flagpole of the Mound Battery under fire on that harrowing Christmas Eve to replace a fallen flag.

Butler did not arrive until the evening of December 24, when the fleet was ending its bombardment for the day. He was angry that he missed the explosion of the powder boat and disappointed that neither it nor the bombardment seemed to have much effect. Reinforced, the ships returned on Christmas Day and pounded the Confederates for hours, reaching a crescendo toward evening, when reportedly 130 shells a minute were falling. That day, the Union fleet fired 10,271 rounds, while the Confederates flung 600 back at them. Porter planned to send his monitors through New Inlet and up the Cape Fear River to bombard the fort from the rear, so he sent boats under the command of Lt. William B. Cushing, who had won notoriety by sinking the CSS *Albemarle* in

October 1864, to sound the approaches. When they were fired upon and driven away by gunners on the Mound Battery, and a shot from Fisher's Armstrong gun hit the boiler of the *Malvern,* Porter's flagship, the idea was abandoned. The passage was not tried again when the Federals returned in January.

Porter was convinced by the relatively weak response from the fort that it had been badly damaged and that the garrison was demoralized or depleted. In fact, only seven guns were disabled by the end of that Christmas Day and Confederate casualties were minimal. Lamb lost just five men killed and thirty-three wounded on December 25. Most of these were among the naval detachment at the Brooke guns, which both exploded, killing and wounding nineteen crewmen. A heavy pall of smoke lay over Fisher as the remaining quarters for the garrison burned, but little other damage had been done. The Federals could not see many men atop the parapets, but that was because Lamb was once more keeping his gunners inside the bombproofs unless they were actually firing their guns.

Encouraged by Porter, Butler ordered Brig. Gen. Adelbert Ames's Second Division of the XXIV Corps, about 3,000 troops, to land north of Fort Fisher on Christmas afternoon. In preparation for this landing, Porter sent Capt. James Alden with the USS *Brooklyn,* which mounted twenty-six large guns, and sixteen other ships to bombard Batteries Gatlin and Anderson. The doughty commander of Battery Anderson, Lt. Col. John P. W. Read of the 38th Virginia Artillery Battalion, had his arm nearly severed by a large shell fragment, and Capt. Thomas J. Southerland of Company I, 1st North Carolina Artillery, took his place. The troops, however, were unnerved by Read's wound, and Southerland could not get them to return to the guns, which included a 32-pounder, two Whitworths, and two field pieces. When Alden reported that the batteries had ceased fire, Butler ordered the 142d and 112th regiments of New York infantry, led by Newton M. Curtis, to land. Three boatloads of sailors outraced the soldiers to Anderson, which they called the Flag Pond Battery, and accepted the quick surrender of seventy-two Confederates, most of whom were from Company A of the 42d North Carolina Infantry.

After the capture of Battery Anderson, the rest of Ames's division landed. Kirkland moved cautiously forward with his two regiments, realized that he was outgunned, and withdrew to a defensive position. Curtis's men approached Fort Fisher under cover of the naval bombardment, but they did not receive orders to attack. When his 117th New York Infantry moved to occupy the road from Fisher to Wilmington, it received an unexpected bonus. As night approached, Major Reece walked into Union picket lines and offered to surrender the 4th and 8th Battalions of Junior Reserves. His youths were tired and hungry, and he did not wish to suffer any more casualties outside the fort. The Federals reported the capture of ten officers and 218 men near Battery Gatlin, which the Union invaders referred to as the Half Moon Battery, but in fact four of the Junior Reserve officers later escaped as well as some of the young men.

Curtis advanced to within fifty yards of Fisher, and Lt. William H. Walling of the 142d New York Infantry won a Medal of Honor by slipping through a gap in the landface palisade to grab a Confederate battle flag that had been knocked from the parapet by a shell. Curtis was eager to attack, and he sent a courier to the landing area to ask for reinforcements to assault the fort. When they did not come, he went himself to the rear and was stunned to learn that none were coming because a withdrawal had been ordered. Twice he sent a courier to Butler to report that the fort could be taken, and each time the answer was the same. Weitzel had told Butler that an attack would be unwise, and the commanding general was clearly inclined to agree with him.

Before making a final decision, Butler dispatched Col. Cyrus P. Comstock, Grant's engineering officer, to take another look at the fort. Comstock went to the front line with Curtis. They had agreed that Curtis should disobey orders and assault with his brigade when the Federal bombardment ceased and the walls were suddenly filled with riflemen and gun crews, yelling and firing at the Union troops. Lamb, understanding that the end of the rain of shells might mean an assault was coming, had ordered half of his garrison to mount the parapets, while he sent the rest to the palisade in front of the land-face. Only one of his guns had been disabled on that side; the rest were loaded and ready for an attack. At the same time, Lamb had his pair of Napoleons run out of the landface sally port to pepper the Federals with canister. Observing Curtis's sudden hesitation and listening to his renewed demands for reinforcements, Comstock cautiously decided that an assault would be suicidal, and he told Butler this.

Butler rode a troop transport, the USS *Chamberlain,* in close for a look and agreed with Comstock and Weitzel that the fort seemed to be dangerously intact. In his official report explaining his decision not to attack, he said that he had in mind the slaughter in 1863 at Battery Wagner, where many of his troops had fought, and Port Hudson, where Weitzel had led a division. Both of these bloody assaults had proven futile. Confederate prisoners also alarmed Butler with their insistence that several brigades of Hoke's division had already arrived and their comrades would soon be coming. Determined that he would not be responsible for a debacle, Butler steamed away, ignoring his instructions from Grant to initiate a siege if an assault failed. Curtis was angry when the order came to withdraw, but worse was yet to come. He and his brigade remained on the beach through that night and the next, shivering in the cold dampness. On the morning of December 27, they were evacuated by the navy; Butler already had started back to Virginia without them.

Losses on both sides in December 1864 were relatively light. The Federal navy lost twenty killed and sixty-three wounded. Of these, half fell when six of their 100-pounder Parrott rifled guns burst while firing. The Confederates also badly damaged four Union ships. The Columbiad on the Mound Battery put a shot through the boiler of the *Mackinaw,* a double-ender serving in Porter's third line of battle, and the *Malvern's* boiler was hit by Fort Fisher's Armstrong gun. Lamb told his gunners to concentrate on wooden vessels; both the *Powhatan,* a side-wheeler, and *Osceola,* another double-ender, were holed below the waterline. Yet another Union double-ender, the *Pontoosuc,* took a hit that forced it out of line for a time, though it returned to the fight. Of about 3,000 troops landed by Butler, 3 were killed and 15 wounded in the sporadic fighting on the beach. Lamb had approximately 1,431 effectives, of whom he lost 6 killed and 55 wounded. Sadly, some of the dead were Junior Reserves, and several hundred more of these young men had been taken prisoner along with Company A of the 42d North Carolina Infantry. Hoke's losses also included about 50 more killed, wounded, and captured from Kirkland's brigade and an unknown number from the Senior Reserves, though some had certainly been killed. Seven of Lamb's guns had been dismounted or damaged, but most were quickly repaired.

Butler had failed, but the Federals were not through with Fort Fisher. In early January 1865, Butler was relieved as commander of the Department of Virginia and North Carolina. Too, Weitzel was removed as commander of the XXV Corps while preparations were made for a return to Fisher. For the Confederates, Whiting and Lamb realized that they had not seen the last effort to take the earthwork, and they frantically demanded more cannon, ammunition, mines, and even hand grenades. None came. Their department commander, Bragg, apparently did not expect another assault. Not only did the general not support the calls for more men and supplies, but he also withdrew Hoke's division, which arrived later, to the city and held a grand review. He even planned to send Hoke's troops back to Virginia. It was Bragg's refusal to accept reality that would make it impossible to hold Fort Fisher when the Federals returned in January 1865.

5

THE MONSTER RETURNS

SECOND ASSAULT ON FORT FISHER, JANUARY 13–15, 1865

Lt. William Calder, the young adjutant of the 1st North Carolina Heavy Artillery Battalion, wrote to his mother on December 20, 1864: "The fleet has come . . . that long-talked-of, much-dreaded monster now lies calmly at anchor off Ft. Fisher, and any hour may see the commencement of the siege so full of . . . woe to us." Calder's concern proved groundless in December 1864, but in January 1865 Fort Fisher became the focus of a more concerted Federal effort. Rear Adm. David D. Porter told Lt. Gen. Ulysses S. Grant that the failure of the first expedition was due to Maj. Gen. Benjamin F. Butler's incompetence. The angry seaman added that an attack by the same troops would succeed if led by a competent officer. Grant was now interested in having a coastal base for Maj. Gen. William T. Sherman's march into North Carolina, so he improved upon Porter's suggestion. An enhanced force, under the command of Bvt. Maj. Gen. Alfred H. Terry, returned less than a month after Butler sailed away. This time, Porter's bombardment was more accurate, and Terry launched his attack on January 15, 1865. The defenders of Fisher, overwhelmed by the greatest naval bombardment of the Civil War, found it impossible to repulse the determined and more numerous Federals.

Porter had greater faith in Terry than Butler, and Grant provided the new leader of the army contingent for the combined operation with more support. The landing force was reinforced to 8,897 troops, including forty-four cannons and mortars. Brig. Gen. Adelbert Ames returned with his Second Division of the XXIV Corps, and another brigade, Col. Joseph C. Abbott's 2d Brigade, First Division, XXIV Corps, was temporarily assigned to him as well. Abbott also brought six companies of the 16th New York Heavy Artillery. Three more batteries of the 1st Connecticut Heavy Artillery were added too, along with three companies of the 15th New York Engineers. The latter joined because Terry was informed that if his assault failed, he was to entrench on Confederate (Federal) Point and await instructions from Grant himself. As before, the army transports were escorted to North Carolina by Porter's fleet, reorganized as a force of sixty ships mounting 611 guns.

The Federal fleet approached Fisher during the predawn hours of January 13, 1865, and began shelling the fort after daylight. This time the Confederates scored the first blow, a harmless hit on the *New Ironsides,* while Lamb's wife resumed her observation point on the far side of the Cape Fear River with binoculars. Unlike Butler, Terry allowed no delay of a few days between the beginning of the bombardment and the disembarkation of troops. Only hours after the first shells fell on Fisher, Federals began landing between the earthwork and Sugar Loaf, to which Maj. Gen. Robert F. Hoke hastily returned with his division. His pickets did clash with the Federals, and Col. John T. Loftin of the 6th Georgia Infantry was killed, but not until the afternoon of January 13 after almost all of the invaders had been safely landed. To add insult to injury, the attackers captured the garrison's cattle, which were promptly slaughtered and cooked.

Abbott's brigade was assigned to guard the stores of the Federal force on the beach, then the rest of Terry's brigades marched south on the night of January 13 to locate a good site for a defensive line to screen an attack on the fort. The march was difficult in the dark, but by two in the morning, Brig. Gen. Charles J. Paine's Third Division, along with two of Ames's brigades, had found a suitable place near Battery Anderson and pushed west to the Cape Fear River. By eight in the morning on January 14, a strong line of trenches was completed and Union artillery began landing. These cannons, which included twenty Parrott rifled guns that could fire thirty-pound shells, four 100-pounder Parrotts, and twenty mortars, were in place by evening, facing Hoke's troops. In the meantime, Bvt. Brig. Gen. Newton M. Curtis pushed his First Brigade toward Fisher, hindered only by shells from the CSS *Chickamauga.* The next day the USS *Nereus,* firing across the peninsula in tandem with the land guns, kept the pesky Confederate gunboat at bay.

While the Federals acted decisively within the careful plans of Terry and Porter, the Confederates floundered. Department commander Gen. Braxton Bragg had sent Hoke's division, which numbered over 6,000 men, to Sugar Loaf. From that point, Hoke's troops could march down the bank of the Cape Fear River to within a hundred yards of Fisher without being seen by warships on the ocean. Bragg also could communicate with the fort by telegraph and had control of the river, which he could use to shuttle his troops. Unfortunately for the garrison, he did not use either route to support them in an effective manner, while the Union troops slipped close to the fort. Bragg's intent never became clear, but he infuriated district commander Maj. Gen. William H.C. Whiting by preparing to evacuate Wilmington even as he ordered Hoke to Sugar Loaf.

Whiting demanded and was given permission by Bragg to go to Fisher on January 13. He dejectedly informed Col. William Lamb that Bragg had decided to sacrifice his garrison and that he wanted to share their fate. Whiting declined Lamb's offer to let him take charge of the post and turned over to Lamb about 600 reinforcements for Fisher's garrison, then about 800 members of the 2d and 3d North Carolina Artillery. Companies D and G of the 3d Artillery waded ashore from a steamer at dark on January 13, watching anxiously as Federal shells fell around them. They joined Companies E and K of the same regiment in the fort. Maj. James Reilly came to Fisher with Companies F and K of the 1st North Carolina Artillery, just as he had during December 1864, and Company D of the 1st North Carolina Heavy Artillery Battalion also returned. They were again joined at Fisher by Company C, 3d North Carolina Light Artillery Battalion, and Company D, 13th North Carolina Light Artillery Battalion. Allegedly there were two companies from the 7th Home Guards Regiment, and the marines and sailors returned to the work. At least fifty marines followed Capt. Alfred C. Van Benthuysen to Fisher, where they fought alongside sixty sailors sent from Battery Buchanan.

Bragg joined Hoke at Sugar Loaf on the night of January 13, then to his "great surprise" found Federals entrenched between them and the fort on the morning of January 14. The 2d South Carolina Cavalry had been posted to report on any attempt by the Union troops to move closer to the fort, but they had failed to detect the movement of thousands of the enemy. After a quick reconnaissance, Bragg decided an attack would fail and bring about the fall of Fisher. He later added in his report that he "did not feel the slightest apprehension for the fort," but he did send some reinforcements. The 7th Battalion and 11th, 21st and 25th regiments of South Carolina infantry, under the command of Col. Robert F. Graham, had been ordered to the western side of the Cape Fear River to support Fort Caswell. On the afternoon of January 14, Bragg sent them to Fort Fisher. After a series of mishaps, Graham landed men from the 11th, 21st, and 25th Infantry at Battery Buchanan. About 350 South Carolinians ran across the open sand under heavy fire to the fort; among them was Pvt. William Greer, who was buried by an exploding shell but was pulled free by a comrade who grabbed his exposed foot. Shaken by such experiences, many South Carolinians dived into bombproofs along the seaface and refused to come out.

Bragg's lack of effective support for the fort became an issue even as the battle developed. He later asserted that he ordered 1,000 troops to the fort and telegraphed Whiting that he expected any assault to be easily repulsed. Whiting only received a fraction of this number of reinforcements and his subsequent reply "greatly disturbed" Bragg. The district commander sent a note to his superior during the afternoon of January 14 informing him that the Federal fleet was "furiously bombarding" Fisher's landface. He declared, "I will hold this place to the last extremity, but unless you drive that land force from its position I cannot answer for the security of the harbor." Whiting may have been exasperated by the apparent

THOMAS YARBOROUGH AND MARTHA HARRELL YARBOROUGH

From Darlington County, South Carolina; Thomas enlisted in Company B, 21st South Carolina Infantry in May 1862, after passage of the conscription act; twenty-nine years of age at the time, with a twenty-two-year-old wife and two children; absent on sick leave for most of summer 1862; rejoined company in November 1862; fought on Morris Island near Charleston in the summer of 1863, when regiment was overrun by Federals on July 10; served with distinction in defense of Battery Wagner until evacuation in September; transferred with regiment in May 1864 to Virginia, where they charged at Walthall Junction on May 6 to stop Maj. Gen. Benjamin F. Butler's advance, then drove his lines back at Drewry's Bluff ten days later; took part in Petersburg siege, during which his regiment suffered heavy casualties defending rail lines; sent south with remainder of Brig. Gen. Johnson Hagood's brigade in December 1864; arrived in time for second Federal attack on Fort Fisher, January 15, 1865; captured when garrison surrendered; died of pneumonia in prison camp at Elmira, New York, on April 28, 1865.

ignorance of those outside of Fort Fisher regarding the situation. This lack of information was made bitterly apparent when a Confederate steamer, the *Isaac Wells,* was captured when it attempted to dock at a landing held by the Federals about a mile north of Fisher. The crew of the Confederate gunboat *Chickamauga,* allegedly incensed at this stupidity, sank the captured vessel with a broadside.

Whiting correctly observed that the Federal bombardment on January 14 and 15 surpassed that of the preceding month in its accuracy and methodical focus on the landface. For his second try at the fort, Porter shuffled his vessels, increasing the firepower of his first line of battle against the landface and Northeast Bastion, and also moved his monitors closer. He added more fire as well on the Mound Battery from his third line of battle. The Union ironclads were especially effective, steaming close to throw shells on Fisher's parapets both day and night. The Confederate return fire was even more sporadic than in December. Lamb had received no resupply since the first engagement, so he had just 2,328 rounds. He thus ordered each gun to fire only once every half hour unless an inviting target approached too close, thus saving his ammunition for an assault. Unfortunately, the Federal bombardment destroyed almost every gun in Fisher before the attack came. At times the garrison did make it hot for Porter's warships. Chief Quartermaster Daniel D. Stevens earned the Medal of Honor for replacing the flag of the monitor USS *Canonicus* several times under fire, but the Union fleet did not sustain as much damage in January as they had in December.

Lamb expected Bragg to take full advantage of the cover of darkness and attack the Federals when their warships could not support them. The commander of Fort Fisher led a small force out through the sally port in the landface on the night of January 14 and engaged Federal pickets. If Bragg advanced, Lamb intended to assail the Union line from his side. For this, he had five of his own companies from the 2d Artillery, the four from the 3d Artillery that had come, and Company D of the 1st North Carolina Heavy Artillery Battalion. They skirmished with the Federals along the river through the night, but there was no effort from Bragg. Disappointed, Lamb pulled his troops back into the fort before daylight on January 15, hotly pursued by shells from the Union fleet.

By January 15, the ongoing bombardment of three days—as many as a hundred shells a minute sometimes fell—had killed or wounded several hundred defenders. A few gaps were filled by the arrival of some of the South Carolina troops, but these learned that almost all of the guns on the landface had been dismounted. Lamb later admitted that Bragg was probably correct that Fisher, as originally built, could have successfully resisted a Union attack. However, while twenty heavy cannons, three mortars, and a trio of Napoleons had been placed to defend the landface, only one Columbiad and the three Napoleons were not disabled by Union fire. The palisade that shielded the landface was riddled with holes, and the electric

MURDOCK H. SMITH

From Bladen County, North Carolina; enlisted at the age of twenty-eight in Company H (Clarendon Guards), 2d North Carolina Artillery (36th North Carolina State Troops) at Elizabethtown in May 1862; assigned to Fort St. Philip in Brunswick County; transferred with company to Fort Fisher in 1864; remained at Fisher during Union bombardments of December 1864 and January 1865; company sortied from fort on the night of January 14, 1865, under the command of Col. William Lamb; formed into skirmish line and advanced until they made contact with the Federals; returned to Fisher when Bragg failed to attack rear of Union lines; Lamb's plan for an assault by Company H and nine other companies of the garrison then canceled; captured when Fort Fisher fell on January 15; sent to Point Lookout, Maryland; released in June 1865 under terms of general parole; apparently settled in Sampson County, North Carolina.

wires to buried mines were "ploughed up." The overwhelming rain of shells forced Lamb to put all of his men in bombproofs, except some sharpshooters, the gunners for the 10-inch Columbiad on the Northeast Bastion, and those for the Napoleon on the far left, where the road from Wilmington entered the fort at Shepherd's Battery. Too, his 8-inch rifled Blakely remained in service upon the Northeast Bastion. When told, its crew would scuttle from cover, quickly load and fire, and then run back. Under such conditions, Lamb's gunners did almost no damage to the Federal warships again on January 15.

The bombardment suddenly stopped that afternoon, and every ship in the Union fleet sounded its steam whistle as a signal for an assault. Realizing that he was outnumbered, Whiting sent a last appeal to Bragg for help. Bragg responded by ordering Whiting to report to him at Wilmington that evening for a conference, as he had told him to do earlier, and by informing him that he had been replaced with Brig. Gen. Alfred H. Colquitt as commander of the district. It was a disappointing reply, and Whiting did as he had done before: ignored it. In the meantime, Lamb had the two Napoleons at the central sally port, which were crewed by Capt. Zacharias T. Adams's Company D, 13th North Carolina Light Artillery Battalion, rolled out to fire upon the attackers. About a hundred South Carolinians from the 21st and 25th Infantry were placed nearby for service in detachments on the palisade as sharpshooters. After sending Major Reilly with 250 men to the left end of the landface, Lamb joined Whiting and about 500 men at the Northeast Bastion, where he thought the main attack would come.

The Northeast Bastion did not receive the primary Federal assault, but it was the focus of an attack by 1,861 Union seamen and 400 U.S. Marines. This unusual assault was adopted because Terry found that what he thought was a pond in the center of his defensive line was actually only a shallow depression. He had to detail more men to cover this wide gap, thus reducing his attacking force. Porter was eager for his own men to participate in an attack, and many of his sailors volunteered to charge Fisher. The naval

detachment was organized into four divisions by its commander, Lt. Comdr. K. Randolph Breese, who also served as
Porter's fleet captain, and careful plans were laid to assault
in three waves. Lt. Samuel W. Preston, who had been one of
the three who ignited the powder boat in December 1864,
led the first division forward to dig rifle pits, which were
quickly occupied by marines assigned to provide a covering

SAMUEL C. WILLIAMS

Enlisted Martin County, North Carolina, August 1862, Company G
(Kennedy Artillery), 2d North Carolina Artillery (36th North Carolina State
Troops); unit became Company D, 13th North Carolina Light Artillery

when it officially transferred to Confederate
service in November 1863 at Topsail Sound on
the North Carolina coast; assigned to Fort
Fisher in the summer of 1864; posted at
Battery Gatlin to the north of the fort; moved to
Batteries Bolles and Purdy on the seaface of
Fort Fisher in November 1864; some of company crewed two rifled guns at Battery Bolles
and the Armstrong rifle at Battery Purdy during
Union bombardment of December 1864; others were assigned to two Napoleons at the
sally port on the landface to meet an anticipated Union assault; Company D returned to Fort
Fisher in January 1865, when the Federal fleet
reappeared; almost all of unit captured with its
guns and horses during main Union attack on
January 15; Williams apparently escaped; hospitalized at Wilmington
with podagra in February 1865; sent to hospital in Goldsboro, North
Carolina, when Wilmington fell later that month; not clear if he rejoined
comrades for battles at Kinston and Bentonville, where battalion lost
almost half of its remaining effectives in just a few minutes; survivors,
including Williams, paroled with rest of Gen. Joseph E. Johnston's army
in April 1865; settled in Windsor, Washington County, North Carolina;
died February 11, 1908, at the age of sixty-three.

fire for the sailor's attempts to board the Northeast Bastion.

Breese's careful preparations were forgotten when the order came to charge. The sailors, joined by marines, rushed across 600 yards of open sand as a disorganized mob. They approached along the beachfront, avoiding the mines buried before the Northeast Bastion but exposing themselves to fire from the Mound Battery. When they approached the palisade, they were met by "a murderous fire of grape and canister" from the Blakely gun and a "galling fire" from Adams's Napoleons at the sally port. Lamb, who barked orders from the parapet until a gunshot through his coat prompted him to adopt a safer position, ordered a volley at 150 yards. It felled

SAMUEL W. PRESTON

Native of Canada; attended U.S. Naval Academy; assigned to fleet at Charleston after graduation; captured in attack on Fort Sumter; imprisoned in South Carolina for a year; volunteered to serve as officer on the USS *Louisiana,* which was filled with powder and exploded, with almost no effect, near Fort Fisher in December 1864; allegedly proposed naval assault on Fisher as part of main Federal attack in January 1865; a participant recalled that the volunteers for this effort, "Sailor-like. . ., looked upon the landing in the light of a lark, and few thought that the sun would set with a loss of one-fifth of their number"; assigned to lead first division of naval force to prepare rifle pits for Marine Corps sharpshooters and clear obstructions; struck in left thigh by minié ball, which ripped open femoral artery, as he approached the Northeast Bastion of Fort Fisher on January 15, 1865; just twenty-three years of age, Preston bled to death on the field.

the first rank and most of the remaining seamen sought cover. They got up but were hit again 100 yards from the fort. Preston was killed along with many others, among whom was Lt. Benjamin H. Porter, his classmate from the U.S. Naval Academy and the commander of the USS *Malvern,* the Union flagship. The survivors pressed forward until enemy fire forced them to seek shelter again. A few passed the palisade, led by Lt. Comdr. James Parker of the USS *Minnesota.* Only one, an English gunner from the USS *Tacony* named James Tallentine, reached the parapet, where he was shot. Parker and Breese lived, but their efforts to organize another assault dissolved into a panic-stricken retreat by the sailors, who left more than 300 casualties behind.

Whiting, like Lamb, climbed upon the parapet as the Union sailors charged, shouting encouragement to his men and defiance to the enemy. After the sailors retreated, both Whiting and Lamb were surprised to see that the Federals had gained a foothold on the works to the far left of the landface. While the seamen had provided a diversion, Curtis's First Brigade spearheaded the main attack by Ames's Second Division. The 112th and 142d New York Infantry led the advance as they had in December, this time driving for the sally port in the landface. Curtis marched in the front rank despite the fact that he and Ames were feuding bitterly over the December withdrawal. Curtis thought Ames had not fought hard enough for an assault; Ames in turn told Terry that Curtis was not suited to lead the advance, though Terry disagreed. Behind Curtis and aligned so they extended farther to the right was Col. Galusha Pennypacker's Second Brigade, while Col. Louis Bell's Third Brigade followed with their right on the river. Abbott's brigade moved down the peninsula from the landing site where they had guarded supplies and waited on the right side of Paine's line as a reserve.

The fire from the Napoleons at the sally port pushed Curtis's troops to their right, and the mass of Federals overran the small Confederate force posted on the left end of the landface. Lamb had ordered the South Carolinians to follow Major Reilly's troops to his left, but most had not. Capt. Kinchen J.

Braddy, commander of Company C, 2d North Carolina Artillery, was in charge of Shepherd's Battery on the extreme left end, where the Wilmington Road entered the fort. The position's two siege guns had been dismounted, but Braddy had the Napoleon at the gate and a Parrott rifle in the gap between his gun chamber and the river to sweep the road and guard the battered bridge that provided access to the earthwork. Unfortunately, the gunners for these pieces, a detail from Adams's company, refused to leave their bombproof, and the mines placed to disrupt an assault failed to explode. Braddy sent some of his own men to the two guns, followed by others

KINCHEN J. BRADDY

Born Cumberland County, North Carolina, 1831; began Civil War as a member of Company F, 1st North Carolina Infantry (Six Months); fought at Big Bethel, Virginia, June 1861; joined Company C, 2d North Carolina Infantry, in February 1862 as a lieutenant; promoted to captain, August 1862, when predecessor resigned; came to Fort Fisher with Col. William Lamb during the summer of 1862; sent to Savannah as part of five-company detachment under command of Maj. James M. Stevenson, fall of 1864; fought at Harrison's Old Fields, December 1864; returned to Fort Fisher after Union attack that same month; posted with his company at Shepherd's Battery to defend the gate where the road from Wilmington entered the post at the river terminus of the landface; driven from position by combination of Union attack, rifle fire from South Carolina infantry, and artillery shells lobbed by Confederate guns at Battery Buchanan and the Mound Battery; defended perimeter around main magazine until overwhelmed; imprisoned at Fort Columbus in New York until exchanged in March 1865; settled on a farm near Fayetteville in Cumberland County, North Carolina, and married; died at the age of seventy-seven in Bladen County, August 20, 1908.

from Company D, 1st North Carolina Heavy Artillery Battalion. Both suffered heavy casualties as Curtis moved forward; Company D, for example, lost forty of its seventy-five men killed or wounded. Among the fallen was Company D's commander, Capt. James McCormic, who was mortally wounded.

Terry watched as Curtis's First Brigade engaged Shepherd's Battery, then ordered Pennypacker's men forward. As they began, canister from Adams's two Napoleons at the sally port killed all of the color guard of the 47th New York, but the Federals did not pause. Ames joined this wave as they raced for the gate between the left end of the landface and the river. His men swarmed over the handful of Confederates remaining by Braddy's guns and joined in the attack on Shepherd's Battery from both the front and rear, overwhelming the defenders. Less than two hundred men surrendered in Shepherd's Battery after it had been surrounded, with Curtis's brigade in front and Pennypacker's in the rear. It was the flags of these regiments that Whiting and Lamb saw from the Northeast Bastion after the sailors retreated.

The Federals had secured the left end of the landface, but this meant that they had to fight their way up that long line, traverse by traverse. Pennypacker was shot down as he led his men with the flag of the 97th Pennsylvania Infantry, his old regiment, in his hand. The colonel survived and was awarded a Medal of Honor and a promotion to brigadier general, but some of his subordinates were not so lucky. The popular young colonel of the 203d Pennsylvania Infantry, John W. Moore, was killed on the first traverse, while Lt. Col. William B. Coan of the 48th New York Infantry never reached the fort. Curtis, meanwhile, pressed on, despite the mortal wounding of the colonel of one of his own regiments, John F. Smith of the 112th New York. In a short time the Union troops had occupied the first three traverses along the landface as well as the intervening gun chambers.

Just when it seemed that the Federal attack could not be stopped, Whiting personally led a Confederate counterattack along the landface. With the help of Lamb, he assembled about 500 men, including about 100 South Carolina infantrymen, the four companies from the 3d North Carolina Artillery, and individuals gathered from other units. Whiting's force hit the Federals at the fourth gun chamber, where the fighting quickly degenerated into a hand-to-hand melee. The Confederates drove the bluecoats out of that chamber and up the third traverse, where Whiting was shot twice while reaching for a Union flag. Allegedly, the Union soldiers guarding the banner called on him to surrender, and the general responded by yelling "Go to Hell, you Yankee bas-

WILLIAM McCARTY

Pennsylvania native; enlisted at West Chester as a corporal in the 97th Pennsylvania Infantry in September 1861 at the age of twenty-five; assigned to Hilton Head in South Carolina; participated in expedition to Florida in early 1862; returned to Charleston area and participated in operations on James Island, where his regiment suffered heavy casualties in a failed assault at Secessionville on June 16, 1862; evacuated from James Island by July 1862; reduced to rank of private but reappointed as corporal after being severely wounded during the late summer of 1862; returned to James Island in July 1863; took part in siege of Battery Wagner on Morris Island until its evacuation by Confederates; assigned once more to Florida in October 1863; transferred to Virginia in April 1864 to join Maj. Gen. Benjamin F. Butler's forces for the Bermuda Hundred campaign; regiment suffered heavy casualties at Cold Harbor and in Petersburg siege; came to Fort Fisher as part of Col. Galusha Pennypacker's  brigade in December 1864 but did not attack; promoted to sergeant and became color bearer for regiment; wounded during fight for Fort Fisher landface on January 15, 1865; remained with regiment for capture of Wilmington and pursuit of Gen. Joseph E. Johnston; served briefly in occupation of North Carolina; mustered out at Weldon on August 28, 1865.

tards" moments before they fired. The Confederates then abandoned their attack, but several retrieved Whiting, who was taken to the hospital underneath the Pulpit, which was already filled with wounded.

While Whiting and his troops grappled with the Federals along the traverses, Lamb ran out of the earthwork through the landface sally port to survey his parapets. He returned to the fort after making sure that Adams's two Napoleons remained in place. It was then that he learned that many South Carolinians still refused to leave the bombproofs, while some of those who had come out to fight were firing haphazardly into Braddy's position. Furthermore, the naval gunners at Battery Buchanan were shelling the landface, "killing and wounding friend and foe indiscriminately." Many of the officers at Buchanan were later accused of being drunk. The artillery crews they commanded had served on the landface of Fisher until their guns were dismounted by the bombardment. They had subsequently marched to Buchanan and had even begun an evacuation before the order was canceled.

While the fighting around the landface raged, Hoke finally received a welcome order from Bragg to attack the line of Federals between Sugar Loaf and Fort Fisher. Hoke personally led his North Carolina brigades, commanded by Brig. Gen. William W. Kirkland and Col. Hector M. McKethan, forward, and they drove back the pickets of Abbott's brigade and Paine's division despite shelling from the fleet. As the Confederates waited in rifle pits captured from the Federals, though, disappointing instructions came from Bragg: they were to discontinue the advance. The department commander still thought the fort would hold on its own, so there was no reason to attack superior numbers under a bombardment. When a dejected Hoke led his men back to their original line, Bragg reassured himself that he had made the right decision by noting that Hoke's uniform had several holes in it, clear evidence of the horrible fate that he and his men might have suffered if their attack continued. Veterans on both sides would later disagree with this assessment, recalling that Hoke's probe had been feeble at best.

To make matters worse for the garrison of Fisher, the Union fleet resumed its shelling with much greater accuracy, blasting Confederates from the parapets just yards away from the Federal infantry. In addition, the renewed rain of shells killed and wounded almost all of Adams's gunners, and he withdrew his two Napoleons into the sally port. As the Confederates reeled from the revived Federal bombardment, Colonel Bell led his Third Brigade forward, carrying a ramrod as a weapon and a seashell plucked from the tide line for his young daughter in his pocket. He was shot as his men crossed the bridge in front of Shepherd's Battery, but they continued without him across the traverses. He asked to be held up so that he could see his flag on the parapet and then was carried to the rear, where he died the next day.

The fight for Fort Fisher rapidly approached its climax as Bell's troops climbed the walls. In response to their arrival and the resumption of the naval bombardment, Lamb ordered the remaining guns on the seaface, two large smoothbore Columbiads and the two cannon on the Mound Battery, a 10-inch smoothbore Columbiad and a Brooke rifled gun, to fire on the landface. He also found more gunners for the two Napoleons at the sally port, which were run out again and began peppering the Union soldiers on the parapet. When this cleared the area of bluecoats, Lamb, believing that Bragg would attack the Federals in the rear, led another counterattack. He gathered a few hundred men and had them fix bayonets, but he fell, shot in the left hip, as he led them forward. When Lamb went down, his attack disintegrated, and he had to be evacuated to the hospital. There he lay next to Whiting.

Lamb's futile counterattack proved to be the high-water mark of resistance by his garrison. When he fell and was carried away, the last hope of the Confederates for a victory left with him. The major of his 2d North Carolina Artillery, James M. Stevenson, had been knocked off the parapet by a bursting shell and almost paralyzed, so as he lay wounded on the field, Lamb gave temporary command of his forces to Capt. Daniel Munn of Company B, 2d Artillery. Once he was at the hospital and could do so, Lamb sent an aide to tell Major Reilly that he was now in charge of the post. Each officer was admonished to continue the fight, for Lamb refused to believe that Bragg was not coming. As the sun sank low on the evening of January 15, however, the Confederates' spirits sank with it. Both of their commanders had fallen, and it was quite apparent that Bragg would not intervene to save a fort that he was convinced would stand on its own. One group of Southerners, perhaps eighty in all, surrendered at the sally port around five in the afternoon and were hustled away. The Federals had a death grip on Fort Fisher, and the Confederates were at the threshold of a disastrous defeat.

DANIEL MUNN

Commanded Company B (Bladen Stars), 2d North Carolina Artillery (36th North Carolina State Troops) since its organization in September 1861; came to Fort Fisher with unit in February 1862; company received Whitworth rifled gun (pictured here) from wreck of British blockade runner; led detachment with Whitworth in August 1863 that saved crew of grounded runner and captured Federal landing party; lost Whitworth gun to capture on August 23, 1863, after bombardment of hundreds of shells from Union warships provoked by accuracy of piece; commanded regiment (five companies present) during Federal attack in December 1864 due to absence of Maj. James M. Stevenson; assumed command of regiment (ten companies) on January 15, 1865, after wounding of Stevenson and Col. William Lamb; led fifteen men from Fisher to Battery Buchanan; captured and imprisoned at Fort Columbus in New York City; returned to Bladen County, North Carolina, after exchange; married, established farm, and reared three children; died during a visit to Wilmington in February 1905.

6

SILENT AS DEATH

SURRENDER OF FORT FISHER
AND ITS AFTERMATH

A correspondent for the *Richmond Daily Dispatch* watched the fight for Fort Fisher through binoculars from Wilmington. He could see four flags on the parapet, only one of which was Confederate, and he cheered as it stayed aloft while Federal banners fell. After dark, though, he reported that the garrison had surrendered, adding, "all is still and silent as death; the never-ceasing roar of the ocean is all that is heard." After six hours of bloody combat, the Confederates abandoned Fisher. Pursued to Battery Buchanan, the remaining defenders found themselves trapped and, without any hope of reinforcement, had to surrender. Their defeat meant that Wilmington, through which passed the last lifeline of the eastern Confederacy, was closed. In February 1865 the city itself was evacuated. Two months later, what remained of the Confederate army in North

Carolina surrendered in the field shortly after the capitulation of Gen. Robert E. Lee and the Army of Northern Virginia. Many years afterward, Fort Fisher became a place where survivors from both sides gathered to talk quietly about the battle, resolving bitter postwar controversies.

Maj. James Reilly was given command of Fort Fisher about nightfall on January 15, 1865, by Colonel Lamb, who lay in the hospital bombproof where he was taken after he was shot in the hip. Maj. Gen. William H.C. Whiting lay nearby, suffering intensely but quietly from the two gunshot wounds he received during his counterattack. Urged by both men to try once more, Reilly gathered about 150 troops. With a color bearer from the South Carolinians by his side, he led a last counterattack and

JOSEPH C. SHEPARD

Pender County, North Carolina, native; graduate of University of North Carolina; studied medicine in New York and France; enlisted in Company A, 3d North Carolina Cavalry; soon reassigned as assistant surgeon and transferred to Wilmington; became post surgeon at Fort Fisher in 1864; present during both Federal attacks; was amputating leg of a Confederate soldier during the evening of January 15, 1865, when he learned garrison had surrendered, but Federals allowed him to complete operation before taking him into custody; held on Governor's Island, New York (where this picture was taken); exchanged six weeks after capture; returned to duty with Gen. Joseph E. Johnston's army in North Carolina; paroled at Greensboro in April 1865; remained with his patients another two months; returned to his home in Scott Hill, North Carolina; moved to Wilmington in 1890; appointed three times as superintendent of health for New Hanover County; twice served as surgeon general for United Confederate Veterans; died at the age of sixty-three on March 5, 1903.

was beaten back. Bvt. Brig. Gen. Newton Curtis led the Federals who subsequently captured the remainder of the landface. Curtis himself confronted and struck down the gunner at the last operational Columbiad in that sector. Meanwhile, Lt. Col. Jonas Lyman, who took charge of the 203d Pennsylvania Infantry after Col. John W. Moore was killed, led an advance inside the fort that paralleled Curtis's attack.

Curtis and Lyman flushed Capt. Zacharias T. Adams's remaining gunners out of the sally port in the landface, where they had taken refuge, but Lyman was killed in the effort. Curtis then defied the orders of his division commander, Brig. Gen. Adelbert Ames, to entrench for the night. Instead, he continued to urge his men forward until an exploding shell felled him. His troops believed he was dead and dragged him roughly from the parapet before realizing Curtis was alive. Even while he was recovering from the wound, which cost him his left eye, a coffin was ordered to send his body home because doctors thought he would not live. He survived and was given both a confirmation of his brevet as brigadier general and the Medal of Honor.

Maj. Gen. Alfred H. Terry saw that a final push was needed, so he pulled Col. Joseph C. Abbott's Second Brigade of the First Division out of the defensive line facing Maj. Gen. Robert F. Hoke's idle Confederates and ordered them into the fort; the gap was filled with Lt. Cmdr. K. Randolph Breese's battered navy detachment. At the same time, Terry told Brig. Gen. Charles J. Paine to send the "strongest regiment" of his black troops into the earthwork. Bvt. Brig. Gen. Albert M. Blackman's 27th U.S. Colored Troops thus advanced alongside Abbott's men. Terry had almost wavered in his resolve to finish the fight in one day, but Col. Cyrus B. Comstock, who had come so close on Christmas Day in 1864, urged him to throw Abbott's troops and some of Paine's men into the fort. Terry himself went forward and made sure that Ames put them into the fight instead of having them entrench.

The entry of Abbott's troops into the fort followed by the 27th U.S. Colored Troops proved to be too much for the Confederates. Low on ammunition and aware that his small force was steadily dwindling, Reilly ordered the evacuation of

Lamb and Whiting, as well as many other wounded, to Battery Buchanan. He told those still fighting to make their way to that position as well. Capt. Alfred C. Van Benthuysen had been shot in the head, but he and a squad of his marines carried Lamb

1ST U.S. COLORED TROOPS

Originally designated 1st District of Columbia Colored Volunteer Infantry; recruited from Northern and Southern free blacks and former slaves; organized in summer of 1863 under the command of Col. John Holman;  sent to New Bern, North Carolina, in August 1863 for garrison duty; moved to Portsmouth, Virginia, in fall 1863 and joined with other black regiments as First Brigade, Third Division, Army of the James; raid to Elizabeth City, North Carolina, in December 1863; honored with selection as provost guard at Portsmouth, January 1864; returned to New Bern to build fortifications in February 1864; moved to Virginia coast to support Maj. Gen. Benjamin F. Butler's Bermuda Hundred campaign; suffered first casualties while repulsing an attack near Jamestown in May 1864; assaulted Petersburg on June 15, losing 156 killed, wounded, and missing; lost 21 killed and wounded at Fort Harrison and 124 killed, wounded, and missing at Fair Oaks; Lt. Col. Giles H. Rich assumed command after Colonel Holman was wounded at Fair Oaks; transported aboard USS *Herman Livingston* to Fort Fisher in December 1864, but few from regiment disembarked for aborted assault; returned to Fisher in January 1865; constructed defensive line north of fort across Confederate (Federal) Point peninsula; occupied Wilmington on February 22; pursued Confederates until general surrender in April 1865; occupation duty in Department of North Carolina until discharged on September 29, 1865, at Roanoke Island; triumphant return to Washington in October as regiment was greeted by cheering mob.

and Whiting across the sand to Buchanan. Perhaps one-fourth of the garrison followed the officers to the battery at the end of Confederate (Federal) Point; almost all of the rest were dead, wounded, or already prisoners. Behind them, the Union troops realized the fort was theirs and began to cheer. A signal light transmitted the news to the fleet.

Reilly intended to make a last stand at Battery Buchanan, using the guns of that work to keep the Federals at bay until his men could be evacuated by steamer from the wharf. There was a mile of open sand between Buchanan and the Mound Battery, and cannon could easily disrupt any pursuit. Upon arriving at the battery, however, he found that the naval detachment, under the command of Capt. Robert T. Chapman, had spiked the guns and fled, taking all usable craft with them. As Lamb and Whiting lay contemplating their fate, well knowing that they would soon be prisoners, they were suddenly interrupted by Brig. Gen. Alfred H. Colquitt of Hoke's division. Colquitt arrived unannounced and reminded them that he had been sent by Gen. Braxton Bragg to take command of the garrison from Whiting, whom Bragg still assumed had taken charge of Fisher when he landed there on January 13.

Informed of the situation by Lamb, who insisted that he organize a counterattack and seize the fort from its conquerors, Colquitt provided no definite answers. Lamb was convinced that the Union troops were demoralized and disorganized from the fighting and that a single brigade from Hoke's division could easily retake his beloved fort. A report that Federals were approaching appeared to make Colquitt uncomfortable, and he prepared to leave. Lamb declined someone's suggestion that Colquitt evacuate him in his launch to safety, but he did ask the general to take Whiting with him; Colquitt hastily departed without either wounded officer. Obviously, despite Bragg's last orders, there would be no meeting between him and Whiting in Wilmington to discuss the fall of Fort Fisher, and Bragg's choice for Whiting's replacement was no longer interested in the job.

While Lamb spoke with Colquitt, the fate of Fort Fisher's garrison was being decided. Accompanied by Terry and

Comstock, Abbott swept the seaface down to the Mound Battery with the 7th New Hampshire Infantry and the 6th Connecticut Infantry followed by the 27th U.S. Colored Troops. Capt. J. Homer Edgerly of the 7th New Hampshire scaled the Mound Battery and took the Confederate colors, but his comrades found only a few prisoners and decided to advance to Battery Buchanan. At the same time, Major Reilly realized his men could no longer fight, so he went with Captain Van Benthuysen and Maj. James H. Hill from Whiting's staff to surrender to the advancing Federals before there was more bloodshed. He found a detachment from Abbott's brigade led by Capt. Charles H. Graves, a member of Terry's staff. Graves agreed to take Reilly and Van Benthuysen to Terry, but on the way they met Abbott's skirmishers under the command of his assistant adjutant general, Capt. E. Lewis Moore of the 7th Connecticut Infantry. Reilly gave his sword to Moore in the traditional gesture of surrender. Soon after, Terry arrived and Reilly's surrender was formally accepted. (Moore kept Reilly's sword but returned it in 1894, one year before the old Confederate died.)

In the confusion at Battery Buchanan, there were other Confederate surrenders. General Blackman of the 27th U.S. Colored Troops in his official report declared that he was the first to receive the surrender of the garrison. As he approached Battery Buchanan in the dark, he halted his regiment and sent forward a detachment. They heard the sound of boats, probably Colquitt and his escort escaping from a nearby wharf, but they ignored these and focused on the Confederates remaining in the battery. In response to a summons from the Federals, Major Hill, who had been left behind by Reilly, advanced and surrendered the troops at Buchanan. The commander of the Union detachment, Lt. Albert G. Jones, later met with Lamb and Whiting and assured them that he would take care of them. Whether Blackman or Abbott first received the surrender of Fisher's defenders became irrelevant about midnight, when Terry reached Battery Buchanan and Whiting, as the highest-ranking Confederate officer, surrendered the garrison to him while lying on a litter. About 500 Confederates were killed and wounded in January 1865, and most of the surviving members of the garrison became prisoners. Of more importance was the closing of Wilmington and the loss of the South's last lifeline.

While the loss of Fort Fisher was a tremendous blow to the Confederacy, it cost the Federals dearly as well. An accident on January 16 increased Federal casualties. Near dawn, 13,000 pounds of powder in Fisher's main magazine exploded, killing more than 200 Federals and their Confederate prisoners. Rumors flew that it was a plot by Lamb, but in fact it was carelessness by two drunken sailors who were exploring with a torch. Ironically, Lt. Henry Benton of the 2d North Carolina

JAMES H. HILL

Son of U.S. Army officer; graduated from West Point in 1855; served as lieutenant, 10th U.S. Infantry; resigned 1861; appointed as assistant adjutant general to Brig Gen. Bernard Bee (with whom he served in Utah before the Civil War); both wounded at First Bull Run, Bee mortally; after recovery reassigned to staff of Maj. Gen. William H. C. Whiting; promoted to major; hospitalized at Wilmington in the spring of 1863; returned to duty as Whiting's chief of staff; came with general to Fort Fisher during Union attack in December 1864; returned again with him to Fisher during assault on January 15, 1865; accompanied Whiting after he was wounded and evacuated to Battery Buchanan; made surrender arrangements with detachment from 27th U.S. Colored Troops; led Col. Joseph C. Abbott to meet with and arrange safety of Whiting; held at Fort Columbus in New York City until paroled in March 1865; returned to Wilmington; received executive pardon from Pres. Andrew Johnson in June 1867; worked for railroad company; died June 6, 1890.

Artillery had earlier been cornered in the magazine with his men when Fisher was overrun. Ordered to come out, he had responded, "Shoot and be damned to you, and we'll all go to Hell together." Cooler heads prevailed at that time, and Benton became a prisoner. The losses from the explosion were added to the totals for the expedition, which were never reported accurately. According to different sources, the Union infantry lost from 814 to 1,234 men killed, wounded, and missing. At the same time, 393 sailors and marines were killed and wounded, most of them in the assault on January 15. It has been noted that it probably cost the Federal attackers one man for every defender in Fort Fisher.

While Federals labored with the monumental task of burying the dead in Fort Fisher, their Confederate prisoners were loaded aboard two steam-powered transports, the *De Mollay* and *General Lyon,* at Battery Buchanan. The sick and wounded enlisted men went to the prison camps at Point Lookout in Maryland or Fort Delaware to wait for the end of the war, while the able-bodied enlisted men went to Elmira in New York. The officers went to Fort Delaware or to Fort Columbus in New York City. Many enlisted men died from injuries or from exposure and starvation while in prison, but most of the officers were exchanged during March. The majority went home, but Van Benthuysen returned to service and accompanied Jefferson Davis on his flight through the South after the fall of Richmond. Not all of the officers came back; Whiting was recovering from his wound at Fort Columbus when he died suddenly of dysentery on March 10, 1865, and Maj. John M. Stevenson, Lamb's second in command for the 2d North Carolina Artillery Regiment, died at the same prison nine days later. Lamb was left to recover at Fort Monroe, where he was confined until May 1, 1865. The wound in his left hip forced him to use crutches for seven years.

Union troops scoured the sands of the battlefield for souvenirs and other loot, while the flag from the Mound Battery captured by Captain Edgerly was presented to a gleeful Secretary of War Edwin M. Stanton when he toured Fort Fisher on January 16. But Federal commanders were interested in bigger prizes. As they expected, their gallantry at Fort Fisher was generously rewarded. Terry's earlier brevet as a major general of volunteers was confirmed, and he was also made a brigadier general in the regular army. Too, he became one of only fifteen officers to receive the thanks of Congress during the Civil War. Ames was brevetted a major general, while Curtis and Pennypacker became brigadier generals with brevets to major general and received Medals of Honor, a decoration also awarded to six comrades of lesser rank who fought at Fort Fisher during January 1865. Colonels Comstock and Abbott were both brevetted brigadier generals. Finally, Paine, the commander of the black troops that stood between Hoke and the fort, was brevetted a major general for his services.

With the fall of Fisher, General Lee lost both a magnificent gift and the war. A few days after the Union victory, the *Owl,* a blockade runner commanded by John N. Maffitt, tried to slip into Wilmington. Aboard was Thomas Conley, a member of the British Parliament, who carried a "full set of horse equipments, saddle, bridle, &c." for Lee and each of his staff officers. Maffitt fled with his ship, but he put the British lawmaker ashore without his gifts for the Confederate high command. Conley traveled to Petersburg to observe the last days of the Confederacy, oblivious to the fact that the loss of Fort Fisher meant the closing of Wilmington, the ultimate defeat of Lee, and the collapse of resistance to the Federal government throughout the South.

Maffitt understood the consequences of Fisher's fall, as did Lee. The blockade runner sailed for Nassau, where he reported that Wilmington was closed. Five blockade runners changed their plans and tried another port, but three had already left before the news came and were captured in the Cape Fear River. Lee and his men soon received official confirmation of the Union triumph at Fort Fisher. In late January 1865 the thinly clad Confederates shivering in the icy trenches before Petersburg were jolted by the firing of a salute with a hundred shotted guns into their lines. This was the Federals' custom when they won a victory, so Lee knew Fisher was gone, and with it went his last dependable connection with the outside world.

Five days after the defeat, Bragg wrote to his brother Thomas, the former governor of North Carolina and attorney general of the Confederacy, "The unexpected blow which has fallen upon us is almost stunning, but it shall not impair my efforts." If he meant a defense of the useless port of Wilmington, this proved to be untrue. The day after Fisher was taken, Bragg began evacuating other defensive works along the Cape Fear River, all of which had been rendered worthless. On January 17 he ordered the guns and magazine at Fort Caswell to be destroyed as well as earthworks nearby and on Smith Island. The Confederates on the west side of the river gathered at Fort Anderson, across from Hoke's troops at Sugar Loaf on the east bank. For the Federals, Maj. Gen. John M. Schofield took charge, bringing two divisions of the XXIII Corps with him. His men flanked the Confederates out of Fort Anderson, then turned their position on Town Creek. By February 21, the Union army faced Wilmington, and Bragg ordered Hoke to fall back while he abandoned the city. The *Chickamauga, Arctic,* and *Yadkin* were sunk by the Confederates, and smoldering naval stores and commodities spewed a pall of dark smoke over the city as Federals occupied the port on the afternoon of George Washington's birthday.

Controversy attended any discussion of the fight at Fort Fisher both during and after the war. Whiting dictated two official reports after his capture, blaming Bragg for the debacle and demanding an investigation. In Bragg's January 1865 letter to his brother, he admitted, "The responsibility is all mine, of course, and I shall bear it as resolutely as possible." If he had restricted his comments to such words, the debate might not have been so bitter, but he did not. Bragg added that Colquitt told him that he found many of Lamb's troops at Battery Buchanan drunk. Too, Bragg declared that most of the defenders never emerged from bombproofs to fight because they were "too drunk for duty." When this letter later surfaced after Bragg's death, Lamb published an acerbic reply in which he damned Bragg for trying "to take from the dead of Fort Fisher an imperishable renown, and . . . to excuse his desertion of a heroic garrison." Charges of drunkenness, Lamb wrote, were "too absurd to require a denial." Not just Confederates argued; Curtis had to be restrained from assaulting Ames when the latter asserted in a public speech that he did everything while Curtis did nothing at Fisher. Curtis, like Lamb, subsequently wrote a public account that provided a more balanced view.

CHRISTIAN A. FLEETWOOD

Enlisted, 4th U.S. Colored Troops, at Baltimore in 1863; had worked as a clerk in that city; regiment sent to Yorktown, Virginia, in October 1863; participated in expeditions in region; fought in Bermuda Hundred campaign and Petersburg siege; lost much of hearing in left ear in fight at Chaffin's Farm on September 29, 1864, when rifle was discharged too close to his head; recovered and served at Fair Oaks in October 1864 and both attacks on Fort Fisher; did not enter the earthwork until the day after its fall, January 16, 1865, when the gruesome sights he saw made him sick; accompanied regiment as it fought at Fort Anderson and occupied Wilmington in February; contracted typhoid fever in March but followed comrades on horseback as they marched to Goldsboro; ordered by regimental chaplain to Wilmington hospital on March 27, 1865; released on April 17 and returned to Goldsboro, where he  learned that Gen. Joseph E. Johnston had surrendered his Confederate army; regiment remained on garrison duty in North Carolina until it was mustered out in May 1866; hospitalized again in Washington, D.C., during the fall of 1865; suffered hearing loss in right ear from lingering effect of typhoid fever; married in 1869; supported his wife and daughter by working as clerk in War Department; joined militia in District of Columbia in 1880; in 1907 received Medal of Honor for actions at Chaffin's Farm; died at the age of seventy-four on September 28, 1914.

It was a shame that such conflicts briefly obscured the efforts of the soldiers on both sides at Fort Fisher. Happily, Lamb and others founded reunion organizations, and by the late nineteenth century, survivors from both sides were gathering to walk through the ruins and reminisce. Like Lamb and Curtis, many enemies even became friends and visited each other's homes. They were quickly embraced by a national public eager to believe that the bloody divisions of the Civil War were behind them. It was ironic that Fort Fisher, on which the survival of the Confederacy had depended in 1865 and for which so many men had died, became a symbol of peaceful reconciliation. It also became the focus of vindication as well. It was through the work of reunion groups that many veterans received the recognition due to them for their role in either defending or reducing the Gibraltar of the South, the greatest earthwork of its time and the key to the defense of the last lifeline of the Confederacy.

Note: The tables of organization presented in the following appendices are compiled from *The War of the Rebellion: A Compilation of the Official Records of the Union and Confederate Armies,* 130 vols. (Washington, D.C.: Government Printing Office, 1880–1902); *Official Records of the Union and Confederate Navies in the War of the Rebellion,* 30 vols. (Washington, D.C.: Government Printing Office, 1898–1922); Walter Clark, ed., *Histories of the Several Regiments and Battalions from North Carolina in the Great War, 1861–1865,* 5 vols. (Goldsboro, N.C.: Nash Brothers, 1901); Frederick H. Dyer, *A Compendium of the War of the Rebellion,* 3 vols. (New York: Thomas Yoseloff, 1959); Weymouth T. Jordan and Louis H. Manarin, comps., *North Carolina Troops, 1861–1865: A Roster,* 13 vols. to date (Raleigh: North Carolina Division of Archives and History, 1966–); and Johnson Hagood, *Memoirs of the War of Secession* (Columbia, S.C.: State Company, 1910). Where the original records are not clear, the order of battle follows that found in Chris E. Fonvielle Jr., *The Wilmington Campaign: Last Rays of Departing Hope* (Campbell, Ca.: Savas, 1997). Unless otherwise indicated, all units are infantry.

APPENDIX A

Union Land Forces, December 24–27, 1864

Department of Virginia and North Carolina
MAJ. GEN. BENJAMIN F. BUTLER

Expedition Commander
MAJ. GEN. GODFREY WEITZEL

XXIV CORPS

SECOND DIVISION
BRIG. GEN. ADELBERT AMES

First Brigade
BVT. BRIG. GEN. NEWTON M. CURTIS
3d New York, Capt. George W. Warren
112th New York, Col. John F. Smith
117th New York, Col. Rufus Daggett
142d New York, Lt. Col. Albert M. Barney

Second Brigade
COL. GALUSHA PENNYPACKER
47th New York, Capt. Joseph M. McDonald
48th New York, Lt. Col. William B. Coan
76th Pennsylvania, Col. John S. Littell
97th Pennsylvania, Lt. John Wainwright
203d Pennsylvania, Col. John W. Moore

Third Brigade
COL. LOUIS BELL
13th Indiana, Lt. Col. Samuel M. Zent
4th New Hampshire, Capt. John H. Roberts
115th New York, Maj. Ezra L. Walrath
169th New York, Col. Alonzo Alden

Artillery Brigade
16th New York Light Battery, Capt. Richard H. Lee

XXV Corps

THIRD DIVISION
Brig. Gen. Charles J. Paine

Second Brigade
Col. John W. Ames
4th U.S. Colored Troops, Lt. Col. George Rogers
6th U.S. Colored Troops, Lt. Col. Clark Royce
30th U.S. Colored Troops, Lt. Col. Hiram A. Oakman
39th U.S. Colored Troops, Col. Ozora P. Stearns

Third Brigade
Col. Elias Wright
1st U.S. Colored Troops, Lt. Col. Giles H. Rich
5th U.S. Colored Troops, Col. Giles W. Shurtleff
10th U.S. Colored Troops, Lt. Col. Edward H. Powell
37th U.S. Colored Troops, Col. Nathan Goff Jr.
107th U.S. Colored Troops, Lt. Col. David M. Sells

Artillery Brigade
3d U.S. Artillery (Battery E), Lt. John R. Myrick

APPENDIX B

Union Naval Forces, December 24–27, 1864

North Atlantic Blockading Squadron
Rear Adm. David D. Porter

Fleet Captain
Lt. Cmdr. K. Randolph Breese

FLAGSHIP
Malvern, Lt. William B. Cushing

DISPATCH SHIP
Little Ada, Acting Master Samuel P. Crafts

POWDER SHIP
Louisiana, Cmdr. Alexander C. Rhind

DIVISION COMMANDERS
FIRST, COMMODORE HENRY K. THATCHER
SECOND, COMMODORE JOSEPH LANMAN
THIRD, COMMODORE JAMES F. SCHENCK
FOURTH, COMMODORE SYLVANUS W. GODON
IRONCLAD DIVISION, COMMODORE WILLIAM RADFORD

First Line of Battle
Canonicus, Lt. Cmdr. George E. Belknap
Huron, Lt. Cmdr. Thomas O. Selfridge
Kansas, Lt. Cmdr. Pendleton G. Watmough
Mahopac, Lt. Cmdr. Edward E. Potter
Monadnock, Cmdr. Enoch G. Parrott
Nereus, Cmdr. John C. Howell
New Ironsides, Commodore William Radford
Nyack, Lt. Cmdr. L. Howard Newman
Pequot, Lt. Cmdr. Daniel L. Braine
Pontoosuc, Lt. Cmdr. William G. Temple
Saugus, Cmdr. Edmund R. Colhoun
Unadilla, Lt. Cmdr. Frank M. Ramsay

Second Line of Battle
Brooklyn, Capt. James Alden
Colorado, Commodore Henry K. Thatcher
Fort Donelson, Acting Master George W. Frost
Juniata, Capt. William R. Taylor
Mackinaw, Cmdr. John C. Beaumont
Maumee, Lt. Cmdr. Ralph Chandler
Minnesota, Commodore Joseph Lanman
Mohican, Cmdr. Daniel Ammen
Pawtuxet, Cmdr. James H. Spotts
Powhatan, Commodore James F. Schenck
Seneca, Lt. Cmdr. Montgomery Sicard
Shenandoah, Capt. Daniel B. Ridgely
Susquehanna, Commodore Sylvanus W. Godon
Ticonderoga, Capt. Charles Steedman
Tuscarora, Cmdr. James M. Frailey

Vanderbilt, Capt. Charles W. Pickering
Wabash, Capt. Melancton Smith
Yantic, Lt. Cmdr. Thomas C. Harris

Third Line of Battle

Chippewa, Lt. Cmdr. Aaron W. Weaver
Fort Jackson, Capt. Benjamin F. Sands
Iosco, Cmdr. John Guest
Monticello, Acting Vol. Lt. Daniel A. Campbell
Osceola, Cmdr. J. M. B. Clitz
Quaker City, Cmdr. William F. Spicer
Rhode Island, Cmdr. Stephen D. Trenchard
Santiago de Cuba, Capt. Oliver S. Glisson
Sassacus, Lt. Cmdr. John L. Davis
Tacony, Lt. Cmdr. William T. Truxtun

Reserves

A. D. Vance, Lt. Cmdr. John H. Upshur
Alabama, Acting Vol. Lt. Frank Smith
Anemone, Acting Ensign William C. Borden
Britannia, Acting Vol. Lt. Samuel Huse
Cherokee, Acting Vol. Lt. William E. Dennison
Emma, Acting Vol. Lt. Thomas C. Dunn
Eolus, Acting Master Edward S. Keyser
Gettysburg, Lt. Cmdr. R.H. Lamson
Governor Buckingham, Acting Vol. Lt. John McDiarmid
Howquah, Acting Vol. Lt. John W. Balch
Keystone State, Cmdr. Henry Rolando
Lilian, Acting Vol. Lt. T. A. Harris
Maratanza, Lt. Cmdr. George W. Young
Moccasin, Acting Ensign James Brown
Montgomery, Acting Vol. Lt. Edward H. Faucon
Nansemond, Acting Master James H. Porter
R.R. Cuyler, Cmdr. Charles H. B. Caldwell
Tristram Shandy, Acting Ensign Benjamin Wood
Wilderness, Acting Master Henry Arey

APPENDIX C

Confederate Land Forces, December 24–27, 1864

Department of North Carolina
GEN. BRAXTON BRAGG

Third Military District (Cape Fear)
MAJ. GEN. WILLIAM H. C. WHITING

FORT FISHER
COL. WILLIAM LAMB (2D NORTH CAROLINA ARTILLERY)

1st North Carolina Artillery (Companies F and K), Maj. James Reilly

2d North Carolina Artillery (Companies B, E, F, H, K),
Capt. Daniel Munn

3d North Carolina Artillery (Companies E and K), Capts.
Malcom H. McBryde and Daniel J. Clark

1st North Carolina Heavy Artillery Battalion, Company D, Capt.
James L. McCormic

3d North Carolina Light Artillery Battalion, Company C,
Capt. John M. Sutton

13th North Carolina Light Artillery Battalion, Company D,
Capt. Zachariah T. Adams

1st (9th) Junior Reserve Battalion (Companies A, B, C),
Maj. D. T. Millard

4th Junior Reserve Battalion (Companies A, B, C, D),
Maj. John M. Reece

7th Junior Reserve Battalion (Companies A, B, C),
Maj. W. Foster French

8th Junior Reserve Battalion (Companies A, B, C),
Maj. James Ellington

Marine Detachment, Capt. Alfred C. Van Benthuysen

Naval Detachment, Capt. Robert T. Chapman

HOKE'S DIVISION
MAJ. GEN. ROBERT F. HOKE

Kirkland's Brigade
BRIG. GEN. WILLIAM W. KIRKLAND
17th North Carolina, Lt. Col. Thomas H. Sharp
42d North Carolina, Col. John E. Brown
66th North Carolina, Maj. David S. Davis
Unattached Units
2d South Carolina Cavalry, Col. Thomas J. Lipscomb
1st North Carolina Artillery, Company I, Capt. Thomas J. Southerland
8th North Carolina Senior Reserves, Col. Allmand A. McKoy
Detachment, 7th North Carolina Home Guards, Col. James G. Burr

APPENDIX D

Union Land Forces, January 13–15, 1865

Terry's Provisional Corps
BVT. MAJ. GEN. ALFRED H. TERRY

XXIV Corps

SECOND DIVISION
BRIG. GEN. ADELBERT AMES

First Brigade
BVT. BRIG. GEN. NEWTON M. CURTIS
3d New York, Capt. James H. Reeve
112th New York, Col. John F. Smith
117th New York, Lt. Col. Francis X. Meyer
142d New York, Lt. Col. Albert M. Barney

Second Brigade
COL. GALUSHA PENNYPACKER
47th New York, Capt. Joseph M. McDonald
48th New York, Lt. Col. William B. Coan
76th Pennsylvania, Col. John S. Littell
97th Pennsylvania, Lt. John Wainwright
203d Pennsylvania, Col. John W. Moore

Third Brigade
COL. LOUIS BELL

13th Indiana, Lt. Col. Samuel M. Zent
4th New Hampshire, Capt. John H. Roberts
115th New York, Lt. Col. Nathan J. Johnson
169th New York, Col. Alonzo Alden

*First Division, Second Brigade
COL. JOSEPH C. ABBOTT

6th Connecticut, Col. Alfred P. Rockwell
7th Connecticut, Capt. John Thompson
3d New Hampshire, Capt. William H. Trickey
7th New Hampshire, Lt. Col. Augustus W. Rollins

Artillery Brigade

16th New York Light Battery, Capt. Richard H. Lee
*16th New York Heavy Artillery (Companies A, B, C, F, G, K), Maj. Frederick W. Prince

*Temporarily attached to Second Division

XXV Corps

THIRD DIVISION
BRIG. GEN. CHARLES J. PAINE

Second Brigade
COL. JOHN W. AMES

4th U.S. Colored Troops, Lt. Col. George Rogers
6th U.S. Colored Troops, Maj. Augustus S. Boernstein
30th U.S. Colored Troops, Lt. Col. Hiram A. Oakman
39th U.S. Colored Troops, Col. Ozora P. Stearns

Third Brigade
COL. ELIAS WRIGHT

1st U.S. Colored Troops, Lt. Col. Giles H. Rich
5th U.S. Colored Troops, Maj. William R. Brazie
10th U.S. Colored Troops, Lt. Col. Edward H. Powell
27th U.S. Colored Troops, Bvt. Brig. Gen. Albert M. Blackman
37th U.S. Colored Troops, Col. Nathan Goff, Jr.

Artillery Brigade

Bvt. Brig. Gen. Henry L. Abbot

1st Connecticut Heavy Artillery (Batteries B, G, and L),
    Capt. William G. Pride

3d U.S. Artillery (Battery E), Lt. John R. Myrick

Unassigned Units

15th New York Engineers (Companies A, B, and H),
    Lt. Keefe S. O'Keefe

Naval Detachment, Lt. Cmdr. K. Randolph Breese

APPENDIX E

Union Naval Forces, January 13–15, 1865

North Atlantic Blockading Squadron
REAR ADM. DAVID D. PORTER

Fleet Captain
LT. CMDR. K. RANDOLPH BREESE

FLAGSHIP
Malvern, LT. BENJAMIN H. PORTER

DIVISION COMMANDERS
FIRST, COMMODORE HENRY K. THATCHER
SECOND, COMMODORE JOSEPH LANMAN
THIRD, COMMODORE JAMES F. SCHENCK
FOURTH, COMMODORE SYLVANUS W. GODON
IRONCLAD DIVISION, COMMODORE WILLIAM RADFORD

First Line of Battle

Brooklyn, Capt. James Alden

Canonicus, Lt. Cmdr. George E. Belknap

Huron, Lt. Cmdr. Thomas O. Selfridge

Kansas, Lt. Cmdr. Pendleton G. Watmough

Mahopac, Lt. Cmdr. Edward E. Potter

Maumee, Lt. Cmdr. Randolph Chandler

Mohican, Cmdr. Daniel Ammen

Monadnock, Cmdr. Enoch G. Parrott
New Ironsides, Commodore William Radford
Pawtuxet, Cmdr. James H. Spotts
Pequot, Lt. Cmdr. Daniel L. Braine
Pontoosuc, Lt. Cmdr. William G. Temple
Saugus, Cmdr. Edmund R. Colhoun
Seneca, Lt. Cmdr. Montgomery Sicard
Tacony, Lt. Cmdr. William T. Truxtun
Unadilla, Lt. Cmdr. Frank M. Ramsay
Yantic, Lt. Cmdr. Thomas C. Harris

Second Line of Battle

Colorado, Commodore Henry K. Thatcher
Juniata, Lt. Cmdr. Thomas S. Phelps
Mackinaw, Cmdr. John C. Beaumont
Minnesota, Commodore Joseph Lanman
Nereus, Cmdr. John C. Howell
Powhatan, Commodore James F. Schenck
Shenandoah, Capt. Daniel B. Ridgely
Susquehanna, Commodore Sylvanus W. Godon
Ticonderoga, Capt. Charles Steedman
Tuscarora, Cmdr. James M. Frailey
Vanderbilt, Capt. Charles W. Pickering
Wabash, Capt. Melancton Smith

Third Line of Battle

Chippewa, Lt. Cmdr. Aaron W. Weaver
Fort Jackson, Capt. Benjamin F. Sands
Iosco, Cmdr. John Guest
Keystone State, Cmdr. Henry Rolando
Maratanza, Lt. Cmdr. George W. Young
Montgomery, Acting Vol. Lt. Thomas C. Dunn
Monticello, Lt. William B. Cushing
Osceola, Cmdr. J. M. B. Clitz
Quaker City, Cmdr. William F. Spicer
R.R. Cuyler, Cmdr. Charles H. B. Caldwell
Rhode Island, Cmdr. Stephen D. Trenchard
Santiago de Cuba, Capt. Oliver S. Glisson
Sassacus, Lt. Cmdr. John L. Davis

Reserves

A.D. Vance, Lt. Cmdr. John H. Upshur

Alabama, Acting Vol. Lt. Amos R. Langhorne

Aries, Acting Vol. Lt. Frank S. Wells

Britannia, Acting Vol. Lt. William B. Sheldon

Cherokee, Acting Vol. Lt. William E. Dennison

Emma, Acting Vol. Lt. James M. Williams

Eolus, Acting Master Edward S. Keyser

Fort Donelson, Acting Master George W. Frost

Gettysburg, Lt. Cmdr. R. H. Lamson

Governor Buckingham, Acting Vol. Lt. John McDiarmid

Launch No. 6, Gunner Hubert Peters

Lilian, Acting Vol. Lt. T.A. Harris

Little Ada, Acting Master Samuel P. Crafts

Nansemond, Acting Master James H. Porter

Republic, Acting Ensign John W. Bennett

Tristram Shandy, Acting Vol. Lt. Francis M. Green

Wilderness, Acting Master Henry Arey

Appendix F

Confederate Land Forces, January 13–15, 1865

Department Of North Carolina
GEN. BRAXTON BRAGG

Third Military District (Cape Fear)
MAJ. GEN. WILLIAM H. C. WHITING

FORT FISHER
COL. WILLIAM LAMB (2D NORTH CAROLINA ARTILLERY)

1st North Carolina Artillery (Companies F and K), Maj. James Reilly

2d North Carolina Artillery, Maj. James M. Stevenson

3d North Carolina Artillery (Companies D, E, G, K), Capts. James S. Lane, Malcom H. McBryde, George C. Buchan, and Daniel J. Clark

1st North Carolina Heavy Artillery Battalion (Company D), Capt. James L. McCormic

3d North Carolina Light Artillery Battalion (Company C), Capt. John M. Sutton

13th North Carolina Light Artillery Battalion (Company D),
Capt. Zachariah T. Adams
Marine Detachment, Capt. Alfred C. Van Benthuysen
Naval Detachment, Capt. Robert T. Chapman
Detachment, 7th North Carolina Home Guards, Col. James G. Burr

HOKE'S DIVISION
MAJ. GEN. ROBERT F. HOKE

Clingman's Brigade
COL. HECTOR M. McKETHAN
8th North Carolina, Lt. Col. Rufus A. Barrier
31st North Carolina, Lt. Col. Charles W. Knight
51st North Carolina, Capt. James W. Lippitt
61st North Carolina, Col. William S. DeVane

Colquitt's Brigade
BRIG. GEN. ALFRED H. COLQUITT
6th Georgia, Col. John T. Loftin
19th Georgia, Col. James H. Neal
23d Georgia, Col. Marcus R. Ballenger
27th Georgia, Capt. Elisha D. Graham
28th Georgia, Capt. John A. Johnson

Hagood's Brigade
COL. ROBERT F. GRAHAM
7th South Carolina Battalion, Lt. Col. James H. Rion
11th South Carolina, Col. F. Hay Gantt
21st South Carolina, Lt. Col. George W. McIvor
25th South Carolina, Capt. James N. Carson
27th South Carolina, Capt. Thomas Y. Simons Jr.

Kirkland's Brigade
BRIG. GEN. WILLIAM W. KIRKLAND
17th North Carolina, Lt. Col. Thomas H. Sharp
42d North Carolina, Col. John E. Brown
66th North Carolina, Col. J. H. Nethercutt

Unattached Units

2d South Carolina Cavalry, Col. Thomas J. Lipscomb

1st North Carolina Artillery, Company I, (Wilmington Horse Artillery)
    Capt. Thomas J. Southerland

3d North Carolina Light Artillery Battalion, Company A,
    (Northampton Artillery) Capt. Andrew J. Ellis

Staunton Hill Artillery, Capt. Andrew B. Paris

FURTHER READING

Barrett, John G. *The Civil War in North Carolina.* Chapel Hill: University of North Carolina Press, 1963. This standard work includes a chapter on Wilmington and blockade runners followed by one on Fort Fisher that provides a fairly accurate, brief account of the battles.

Butler, Benjamin F. *Butler's Book.* Boston: A.M. Thayer, 1892. Many interesting details can be found in the two chapters devoted to Butler's defense of his actions at Fort Fisher.

Clark, Walter, ed. *Histories of the Several Regiments and Battalions from North Carolina in the Great War, 1861–1865.* 5 vols. Goldsboro, NC: Nash Brothers, 1901. An early effort to provide a history of every Confederate unit from North Carolina, these tomes contain essays mostly written by men who served in the organizations, including those who fought at Fort Fisher. There is also a reprint of William Lamb's article from the *Battles and Leaders* series.

Finan, William J. *Major General Alfred Howe Terry: Hero of Fort Fisher.* Hartford: Connecticut Civil War Centennial Commission, 1965. This biography of the Union commander of the second combined expedition obviously focuses on his sole effort as an independent commander during the Civil War.

Fonvielle, Chris E., Jr. *The Wilmington Campaign: Last Rays of Departing Hope.* Campbell, CA: Savas, 1997. Information from newly uncovered documents enhances this most recent and extensive study of the Federal campaign to capture the eastern Confederacy's last major port.

Gragg, Rod. *Confederate Goliath: The Battle of Fort Fisher.* New York: Harper Collins, 1991. This remains the standard work on the fight for Fort Fisher itself. The research is quite impressive, and the writing is entertaining.

Johnson, Robert U., and Clarence C. Buel, eds. *Battles and Leaders of the Civil War.* 4 vols. New York: Century, 1887. Reprint, New York: Thomas Yoseloff, 1956. Volume 4 contains a first-hand account of Federal naval operations at Fort Fisher and yet another explanation of his defense by William Lamb.

Lamb, William C. "The Battles of Fort Fisher." *Southern Historical Society Papers* 21 (1893): 257–90. The commander of Fort Fisher expands upon the points made in his earlier publications, thanks apparently to the printing of the *War of the Rebellion* series.

_____"Defence and Fall of Fort Fisher." *Southern Historical Society Papers* 10 (1882): 350–68. In this first published defense of his actions and those of his garrison, Lamb includes a copy of Braxton Bragg's slanderous letter of 1865 and refutes it point by point.

Merrill, James M., ed. "The Fort Fisher and Wilmington Campaign: Letters from Rear Admiral David D. Porter." *North Carolina Historical Review* 35 (October 1958): 461–75. Porter made sure that his key role in the campaign was well understood in these letters to Gustavus V. Fox, the assistant secretary of the navy.

Nash, Howard P., Jr. *Stormy Petrel: The Life and Times of General Benjamin F. Butler, 1818-1893.* Rutherford, NJ: Fairleigh Dickinson University Press, 1969. This work contains the most extensive chapter on the Fort Fisher campaign to be found in any biography of Butler.

Official Records of the Union and Confederate Navies in the War of the Rebellion. 30 vols. Washington, DC: Government Printing Office, 1894–1922. Reports and communications concerning the U.S. Navy during the Fort Fisher campaign can be found in series 1, volumes 9–11.

Porter, David D. *Incidents and Anecdotes of the Civil War.* New York: D. Appleton, 1885. Years after the Civil War ended, Porter still had few kind words for either Benjamin F. Butler or his efforts at Fort Fisher.

Price, Charles, and Claude Sturgill. "Shock and Assault at Fort Fisher." *North Carolina Historical Review* 47 (winter 1970): 25–39. The authors provide a detailed discussion of the powder boat scheme.

Reed, Rowena. *Combined Operations in the Civil War.* Annapolis: Naval Institute Press, 1977. The Fort Fisher campaign is presented as a classic example of a combined operation, and the author provides interesting insights on events.

Trotter, William R. *Ironclads and Columbiads: The Coast.* Winston-Salem: J.F. Blair, 1989. This popularized account of events along the North Carolina coast during the Civil War contains a substantial amount of material about Fort Fisher and the role of Wilmington.

The War of the Rebellion: A Compilation of the Official Records of the Union and Confederate Armies. 130 vols. Washington, DC: Government Printing Office, 1880–1902. Reports and communications concerning the U.S. Army during the Fort Fisher campaign can be found in series 1, volumes 46–47.

Wise, Stephen R. *Lifeline of the Confederacy: Blockade Running during the Civil War.* Columbia: University of South Carolina Press, 1988. Extensively researched, this pivotal account of blockade running throughout the Confederacy contains a great amount of information about the role of Wilmington.

INDEX